G000112956

EMPTY W

HALF FULL

EMPTY WHEN HALF FULL

A cantankerous consumer's compilation of
mistakes, misprints and misinformation

PATRICK FORSYTH

bookshaker

First Published In Great Britain 2011
by www.BookShaker.com

This one is for Sue, who punctuates my writing with such phrases as "Knock, knock", "Can you talk?" and "What are you doing?" (in the most delightful way, of course); and hopefully it is to assist the holiday fund.

CONTENTS

ACKNOWLEDGEMENTS

THERE IS A GREAT DEAL of nonsense quoted in these pages, some of it wrong, mistaken, erroneous, inaccurate, misinformed or just plain careless. So, despite the writers' ignorance of either the facts or of the written word (and in many cases, I suspect, both), or indeed their slapdash checking or their sheer duplicity – for there is a good deal here that one fears was *intended* to deceive – I suppose I should thank them. Without their mistakes this book would not exist. Whilst the book revels in the humorous nature of such errors, the prevalence of such weapons of mass disinformation should be challenged and its originators castigated, and indeed that too is one purpose of this book.

I should also say that what is quoted here represents at least a couple of years of progressively collecting items to include in the book. This proceeded by first hand observation of the errors or, more often, of a wide range of places that reported them (including magazines, newspapers, web sites and radio and television programmes). To the best of my knowledge everything in the book is accurately quoted and (perhaps there should be an allegedly in here somewhere) existed at least for a while at some time in the recent past. Of course, some at least of the originators of the material quoted have probably spotted their errors by now and amended their material. This might be because they noticed their mistake or someone pointed it out to them, or because they decided to turn the volume control on their deception down a bit. I hope so.

Some of the mistakes quoted have potentially serious repercussions. Maybe it is one of the offending companies who placed the advertisement below in the hopes of changing matters before the mistake was made. But, however they came about, the mistakes here are chosen primarily for their nonsensical quality and tendency to make us smile, so perhaps we should not regret their passing but rejoice that for a little while they made customers chuckle as they read the material from product providers produced with less care than we – or they – might wish. If reviewing the misdeeds of those featured here teaches us to be less easy to persuade – less gullible even – in future, then serve them right.

A job advertisement in the *Shropshire Star* asks for **"Past Prevention Technician"**

INTRODUCTION

Everything is not as it seems

"In order to discover the truth of an advertisement
it is necessary to read between the lines."

Irving Fletcher

WE LIVE IN A WORLD OF bewildering choice. You can buy almost everything you can think of and a good many things that you cannot. Consider this advertisement from the play.com catalogue:

> *Acre Of The Moon. In stock.*
> *Usually dispatched within 24 hours.*
> *Our price £19-99 Delivered.*

The offer above is surely bizarre (and what method are they using to pack and dispatch, I wonder?), but no more so than many others. We also live in a world in which we are besieged by injunctions to buy; the average person has literally thousands of promotional messages directed at them every day of their lives. Some of this we rail against, some we take for granted and some we like and use.

It used to be said that if you built a better mousetrap then the world would beat a path to your door. No more. Any organisation wanting to survive and profit in a harsh and competitive commercial world must work actively to ensure that customers are informed that their product or service exists and actively persuade them to buy. In most cases this is an on-going process; when we buy once we are encouraged to buy again – and again.

This is true whoever the customer is. Be you in the market for toffees, toothpaste or a new toaster then those who produce such goods will find ways to communicate with you. If a company buys computers, corrugated iron or consultancy then they too will be in receipt of regular communications from those people intent on selling such things.

A guidebook promises to tell:
The real story of the mythical King Arthur.

The volume is staggering. For instance, there are dozens of different brands of toothpaste and the producers of all of them want to communicate with everyone who might buy their product; in the case of toothpaste that includes just about everyone (except perhaps the guy who sits next to you on the train to work). The different forms of media used to accomplish this are many and varied. Advertising is an obvious method, one visible to everyone. Advertisements appear in the press and on radio and television, but they also appear on posters, packs of book matches, pop-ups on your computer screen and on the side of the space shuttle. And more: make a list; it will be a long one.

Though many people tell researchers that they do not like advertising, and take steps where possible to avoid it – who has not zapped through the commercials on a recorded television programme? – people also rely on it. How else would we know what is available? How else would we make a choice between product A and product B? This is certainly not judged solely by price or the cheaper brands would outsell the brand leaders, and they don't. The money leading brands spend on advertising must come from somewhere. It does; it comes from you. Remember that you can always save money by keeping clear of brand leaders and that some of the companies concerned probably make the own brands you might buy instead anyway. Price is a guide, one factor amongst many to be weighed up in order to assess whether something is suitable to buy, but what matters is value for money and fitness for purpose. We buy what we feel will suit us best. Often this involves compromise – or we would all drive a Rolls Royce.

One thing is for sure: what we are told about products and services by their makers is a major influence on buying habits. The information suppliers provide is, or should be, genuinely useful. The image they create can be more important, and is often very powerful. My mother was convinced that my feet would drop off unless clad in Clarke's shoes, though that was, it must be said, many years ago. Brand images are nowadays even more powerful. Products must perform; no one will buy a pair of shoes of the same brand again if their first pair is falling to bits within the hour. But, generally, those who communicate most powerfully sell most.

The names of the major players are well known, often across the world. As you emerge from the airport in almost any major city you see posters projecting the same names: BMW, Sony, Canon, IBM, and more. The name itself must be right; BMW seems to have a strong image, one that it is hard to imagine could have been cultivated so successfully if it had continued to trade under its original name of the Bavarian Motor Company. On the other hand, Smiths sell a very large quantity of potato crisps on the back of what must be one of the most ordinary names in the world, so other communication must be adding something.

Washing instructions label on trousers:
Dry clean only in clean water

Yet despite the imperative of communicating effectively, despite the millions spent on it and despite the professionalism of those who work at making it so, sometimes customer communications fall a tad short of what is intended. I am understating it – some communication is wrong, inaccurate, confusing or devious and much of it so ill-thought about that it just ends up humorous.

It was ever thus: for how many years have chemists and others displayed signs saying *Ears pierced while you wait*? As if there was some other way. Examples still abound. However did it come about that the following messages to customers appeared as shown?

- Sticker inside the boxes in which DVDs are hired: *Please rewind.*
- Electrical goods advertisement: *We offer one of the best finance deals around – 0%.* Well, it would be.
- Sign inside hotel bedroom door: *In the interests of security please close door securely before entering or leaving your room.* It would be a good trick if you could do it.
- A new pill to rival Viagra was launched with a note saying: *Essentially it provides a lot more flexibility than Viagra does,* which presumably labels it as not so good.

These may prompt amusement. They may have you wondering for a moment, but someone wrote all of these, others probably checked them, they were printed and circulated – and, in the case of the penultimate one, it was fastened to all 252 individual bedroom doors in the hotel – yet *still* no one noticed that it appeared in an amusing, confusing and annoyingly incorrect form.

Does it matter? Well, yes, I think it does. Such may sometimes provide innocent amusement for customers, but there is a real danger that their image of the organisation will be diluted as a result. If they are at pains to be thought of as expert, experienced, trustworthy or whatever, can this be so if their communication is seemingly cobbled together without a thought or a check? Can you trust such people? Or rely on their service and products? Should you do so? Specifically:

- Do you want to buy a hot chocolate sachet that says it contains a "*source of milk*"? If they put a whole cow in there, what else do they do?
- Do you want to deal with a bank so inept they email customers saying, "*If you cannot see this email, click here*"? Though, actually, if that is anything to go by you'll never know you are dealing with them
- Maybe it's safer to buy an ice-cube tray described as "*Freezer safe*"; certainly it suggests it is worth avoiding ones that are not.

Incidentally, considering the process of checking (or rather not checking) reminds me of the computer manual with the following boxed paragraph prominent on its title page:

> *This manual has been carefully to remove any errors.*

One feels for whomever proof read this, they could not have missed out a worse word ("checked", of course) – but I digress. Sometimes the nonsense is written at length. Someone has a whole paragraph to realise that something is not exactly making sense. A classic example comes from the film hire company Blockbuster saying:

> *"Limited Time Only. Rentals not returned by noon on date due shall be assessed an extended viewing fee on a per rental period basis, 5 day rentals are now one week rentals and if not received by noon on the 9th day shall be assessed an extended viewing fee equal to the original price for each additional weekly rental period, provided that the extended viewing period fee policy in participating franchise stores may vary... See participating stores for details and extended viewing fee policy."*

I got tired typing it and skipped to the end. Thank goodness you can check the details in their shops, though goodness knows what they were like. I am not sure whether to give this the Gobbledegook of the Year Award for being utterly impenetrable or to give a prize to anyone who can understand it.

This book investigates the vagaries of customer communication in all its forms: from the simplest sales letter that drops through your letterbox to the press release, newsletter, promotional brochure, product literature and advertisements, direct mail and electronic communications too that doubtless besiege you on a daily basis. It looks at how customers can be misinformed or confused, at how claims may be so poorly stated as to become a nonsense and how inaccuracies of every kind can paint a picture of an organisation the very reverse of the kind anyone would want to do business with.

These are not just to do with writing clearly, incidentally; all sorts of things conspire to make things inappropriate. For example, one you will not have seen (it was quickly pulled) is the campaign mounted by the Hong Kong Tourist Board under the slogan *Hong Kong takes your breath away*. It appeared just as SARS (severe acute respiratory syndrome) took hold across the region. Oops. A lucky escape and the timing of such things can be worse.

As a customer – and we are all customers for something – much in these pages may well amuse. It may also get you into the habit of checking and noticing such things, so that you do not find yourself unwittingly buying something from an organisation in which it seems no one can write three words in a row and make them make sense, and wondering if their attitude to service, safety or product reliability exhibits the same lack of care.

In an era where some films are advertised on television highlighting that, "*this film contains mild language*" (a warning of strong language has some recognisable purpose, but how does this help us? Maybe there are people who think we need alerting before we hear the word "bland"), one might say that the following pages contain some rum language. Some qualify as WMDs: weapons of mass disinformation; some just make you wonder how they ever came to be written, like the discount bedding store advertisement which says: *Our January sale only happens once a year.* Presumably as opposed to all those stores who work to radically different calendar. See what you think.

Forewarned is forearmed

Note: The emphasis here is unashamedly on those messages that are inadvertently humorous, but there is still a moral to be taken from looking at this sort of stuff. It just shows how careful you have to be in your purchase decisions. Even the most ambiguous phrase

---

can somehow still often seem impressive, and some people are led to buy or think they have a bargain (or both), when the claim being made has little substance or is out and out nonsense. So the famous Latin legal phrase, *caveat emptor* (which means buyer beware), is one to keep in mind. You can pick up useful purchasing hints here along the way to stop you being deceived and help you get a good deal.

The examples quoted here all make the point that those directing these messages at us are not entirely to be taken at their word, except perhaps whoever put up a mysterious sign saying simply *"UNPUBLICISED SALE"*. That's a contradiction in terms and one you can safely ignore, I would suggest.

INTERLUDE

Say "when"

One ploy that is used to persuade you does not even use words. Consider the way the usage of certain products is presented in advertisements. Toothpaste is a good example: pictures show the amount of paste squeezed onto the brush... and it is always enormous. In television ads the shot always cuts away before the squeeze is finished so you are left feeling that the squeeze goes on and on. It all gives the impression that you must maximise the amount of toothpaste used and the unfinished shot seems destined to end up with the toothbrush so full that it will be almost impossible to get it in your mouth.

Whatever the product, this is an insidious process too; use any smaller amount and we might imagine that it is somehow wrong. They don't actually say, *"What do you call that little smear, think that will even begin to clean your teeth and ban your stinking breath, think again!"*, but somehow they might as well. If we always see such usage this way, we feel it's normal. At worst we might gear up our usage – and the money we spend – by a considerable amount. After all it always used to be said that the makers of mustard made their profit not from the mustard we consume but from the dollops left on the side of our plates. This whole

11

business is true of all sorts of products, but especially of things like sauces of any sort that can be shown flowing – or perhaps gushing is a better word – in abundant profusion to encourage extra spending. Shampoo is another example and this is one of a number of cases where an impression of sensuousness and luxury creeps in as an over-generous pouring of shampoo is shown flowing in slow motion, glistening in all its glory. You may consider all this sneaky; certainly you should try not to have your behaviour altered by it.

It was Oscar Wilde who said that "Moderation is a fatal thing. Nothing succeeds like excess," but this was before consumerism hit present day heights. You are better to use only what you need to use if you want to save money.

1. THE ART OF THE BLEEDING OBVIOUS

Just in case you don't know

"I wish people who have trouble communicating would just shut up."

Tom Lehrer

YOU WOULD THINK THAT ANYONE with a product to sell would respect their customers. Some companies have motivational maxims posted around their offices saying things like "The Customer is King", lest they forget. Yet at the same time they often seem to treat customers with substantial distain. After all, how could anyone who thinks that I like holding on the telephone for a long and indeterminate time, listening to some whining or pounding pop song repeating endlessly and then pushing buttons to work my way through six levels of options only to be told that for that sort of query I should call another number, possibly respect or care about their customers? They. Do. Not. If you detect that I am on a bit of a hobby horse here then you are correct, but I bet it's one you ride too, dear reader.

> A host of premises have notices saying:
> **Only guide dogs are permitted to enter.**
> Luckily for their continued business
> most people seem to ignore them.

Throughout the book, we focus on how customers are communicated with and the inadequacies of much of that communication. Inadequacies run from sheer sloppiness – like the hi-fi shop that sells *"revolving turntables"* – to downright deviousness designed to prompt us to ignore any shortcomings and buy, buy, buy. But here, and in the next chapter, we start with examples of the simple things. These mostly do no great harm, and assuredly many make you smile, but equally they do not paint a picture of wondrous organisations ready to care for you in every way. This may not matter in routine matters – for instance Doom mosquito destroyer mats claim *"Kills mosquitoes for up to 10 hours"* but dead is dead so to speak, so we sort of know what they mean. But consider Frudix (a medicine for cats and dogs) the directions for which state *"One tablet per 10 kilograms once or twice a day at 8 hour intervals"*. I think I want a company in that kind of business to be a little bit more careful and use a little more precision with regard to dosages, so that those with sick animals are sure when to give the next pill. They should definitely go on the naughty step.

Our main theme here highlights those who spell out information we simply cannot do without – actually I mean that we *don't* need. Product producers should not take us all for idiots. Most of us are not; though I just read of someone listening to a radio show which was discussing eclipses. Hearing a warning against looking directly at the sun they phoned in to ask, "If eclipses are so dangerous, why do we keep having them?" There are assuredly some people who need a mental upgrade.

Back to unnecessary statements. For example, *"Pears Herbal Care Aloe Vera, Honeysuckle and Vitamin E Shampoo maintains the health and shine of normal hair – for less than more expensive brands"*. Well I guess they wouldn't be less expensive otherwise. What a name too – I would almost prefer to have hair that was abnormal so that I don't have to use it. Imagine bathing with a friend: by the time you had said "Can you pass the Pears Herbal Care Aloe Vera, Honeysuckle and Vitamin E Shampoo, please", the water would be cold and any romantic moment would have long passed.

While mentioning shampoos I discover that there are special ones made for animals. When I had a dog, I seem to remember, we used one called Fairy Liquid, but there are now special ones. Assisi Tea Tree Concentrated Shampoo is for rabbits and small animals. It sounds irresistible *"Blended with the finest pure plant oils. pH balanced, low lather and non-toxic.*

Suitable for all coats. Gentle on the skin. Acting as a non irritant for those rabbits and small animals with skin problems". Oh joy, I almost wish I was a bunny rabbit and could enjoy it. I do hope it is as good as is suggested and does no harm, as it also says *"Not tested on animals"*. Now animal testing of many things is rightly frowned on, but wait a minute, here they are selling this stuff on the open market, customers are covering little Flopsy or Mopsy in its bubbles and yet they can't give even one of their own pets a quick rinse and make sure it's ok; that seems irresponsible.

Even more blindingly obvious is a Nokia mobile phone leaflet telling its users *"You will need to remove the existing battery if you want to install a new battery."* How long would people fiddle about trying put a new one in without that advice, I wonder.

UK Advanced Hair Studio offers –
Hair Loss Results Guaranteed

Any kind of technological gizmo needs care, even, evidently, the humble telephone. One BT phone comes with this amongst the instructions: *"Situate your product close enough to the telephone and mains supply sockets so that the cable will reach them."* If there really are people who need to be told that, then perhaps they should spell it out fully: "the product is a telephone;

16

the 'mains' refers to electricity". It would be so sad if a customer connected their shiny new phone to the cold water tap in the kitchen. Mentioning BT, the BT Response75 telephone is no longer made, I think, and that might be because its message taking function voiced a cheery, "Thank you for calling," out into the room, but only after the caller had hung up.

Cameras are complicated gizmos these days – some of them make telephone calls and toast too, for all I know – and the digital ones certainly need detailed instructions. The Canon G12 starts by aiming to risk no misunderstanding and says, *"The various types of memory card that can be used in this camera are collectively referred to as memory cards in this guide."* This just makes you long to read the rest of the manual and I confidently predict it will tell you that it refers to buttons as buttons and batteries as batteries.

A door in a school has a sign saying:
This door can only be used when it is unlocked.
Well obviously, but is this is an instruction or part of the pupils' education?

The label on a box containing a coffee mug warns: *"May get hot in microwave"*, which is not quite as stupid as Pampas lemon pudding's label telling you: *"Warning – contents may get hot after heating"*. Both warnings are surely unnecessary, though is there a question posed by their use of the word "may"? Surely these things *will* get hot if you heat them up and if they don't, then... you haven't heated them. Maybe the microwave is not close enough to the electric point to plug it in.

These set the tone and there are so many ways we are taken for idiots. Amongst many other examples of pointing out the obvious, I would mention the following:

- The web site of the charity Optimum Population Trust states helpfully that "*Sex is the main cause of population growth*". It does not mention any other causes.

- Black & Decker masonry drills are evidently designed to "*drill on contact*".

- Five Spice Powder lists only one ingredient and that's "*Five Spice Powder*", which is both obvious yet leaves us wondering what on earth it is made up of.

- Limbitin is a natural remedy of some sort recommended for treating restless leg syndrome. Some medicines are hard to take but this is described as easy to take and says it should be "*consumed orally through the mouth*"; presumably any other form of oral consumption is frowned on and may even do damage – perhaps it would make your leg twitch.

- The warnings on Ambien, a prescription sleeping pill, says "*May cause drowsiness*". Well, so it should. In fact it should surely go way beyond drowsiness if, as another product says in a slogan that seems to have gone into the language, *"it does what it says on the tin"*.

- Aboard a nine-seater passenger plane is the notice: *"The minimum flight crew is one pilot"*.

- The reflecting safety bands produced by Crane Sports for runners training after dark helpfully point out that *"The retro-reflective material and LED light must be on the outside"*.

- A sign in a post office says *"Gas engineers. If an item does not fit in the box do not put it in"*. I am unsure why they should single out gas engineers or indeed why they would think anyone would struggle to put something into a box manifestly too small for it

- The Bosch IX0 electric screwdriver comes taped firmly inside a box. Open the box and the tape holding it in place has printed on it: *"Remove after opening the box"*.

- A Crate & Barrel shelving unit needs assembling after purchase and tells you helpfully *"Note: people are required to safely assemble this product"*; the robot age is still a little way off, then.

- A watch strap is labelled *"To be worn on the wrist"* as if being a watch strap wasn't information enough.

- Puma socks tell you to *"Wash when dirty"* which is maybe only sensible if it is directed exclusively at teenage boys.

All these and more have me tearing my hair and despairing of the very existence of such communications. Do the writers of such things think the public all have the brains of retarded dormice or is it simply that they think hardly at all? I would even take issue with Sony (headphones) explaining that you should *"Wear the earpiece marked (R) in your right ear and the one marked (L) in your left ear"*. It is clear, but is it necessary? Sometimes there is a double twist to this kind of thing. ASDA have shops with in-store opticians in them and one such has a sign saying: *"Contact lens patients should remember to bring their lenses with them or we will be unable to see them"*. Nobody evidently saw the odd way that is put and, anyway, surely if you are the patient without lenses it is more likely that you will be unable to see the optician.

The auction site, eBay, is a marvel of the age and many people now buy many things on it. To help their customers get what they want in the final months of the year they flag the news that *"As Christmas is approaching, the postal service will be very busy recently"*. Oh, was it? Boxes of "Celebrations" chocolates have some printing on the bottom of the box, one part of this says: *"Do not read this whilst box is open"*. Sensible enough, but surely by the time you complete a reading of the sentence your chocolates will be on the floor.

One particular form of promotion is worth a mention here: that of competitions. The purchase of many products qualifies you to enter a competition, and prizes in such things can be lavish and tempting. You should note two things about them. First almost always any question posed is one able to be answered by even the least bright shopper. Something like: "Is 2+2 ... 236, 78 or 4?" So a first reaction is always likely to be *I can do that.* But the second thing to watch for is the use of the beguiling words, "All you have to do...". Suggesting that, for example, all you have to do is answer the question. No it is not all you have to do. You not only have to send in the right answer, you have to be picked out from all the many right answers as the winner. The odds are likely to be thousands to one against you; perhaps hundreds of thousands to one. They really hope that you will fall for this "all you have to do" business and send in an entry. Thousands do and the vast majority win nothing. They just – if they add their email address – receive promotional messages twice a week for the rest of their lives. Be warned.

I could list more, but let's limit it to the following. Even the prestigious *Harvard Business Review,* which is surely read by intelligent people, has an online subscription form that can be completed and paid for by credit card. Linked to its request to set down your credit card number is the note that this is: *"The large numbers across the middle of the card".* Whoever wrote this seems to take a dim view of the level of intelligence of their potential subscribers. Announcements can be as guilty as notices in this respect. One made in Sydney's main railway station is reported to have said: *"Attention, passengers. For your convenience, please arrive at the station before your train is scheduled to depart."* Oh so helpful, except that if you have not done so you presumably not only miss your train, but you miss the announcement too. Perhaps they should also point out that you should not get off the train before it has arrived at your destination.

Seriously... be warned

No great harm is done by things of this sort, but it can be a sign of

i) a lack of respect for the customer
ii) a lack of care in the way an organisation works
iii) that you are about to do business with a blithering idiot.

When you see this sort of thing you may want to double check that the product is all it says it is and that a similar lack of attention is not applied to its supply.

Occasionally you see something like the examples here that makes you wonder if it is not intentional, written not by an idiot, but by someone with a sense of humour well aware of what they are doing. I would like to think that the hospital administrator who ordered a particular sign fixing to a door in the maternity department knew exactly what they were doing. It said: "*Delivery Room – Push*".

So much for things falling into the "obvious trap"; let's move on. The next chapter adds some ambiguities and the following one considers things that are frankly just impossible.

INTERLUDE

Nonsense from the senses

In addition to what we are told about products, a variety of other tactics are used to persuade us to feel sufficiently positive about them to buy. Here, just let me point out some of the utterly illogical ways in which we respond and thus how these influences are brought to bear.

Take French wine. You may like it. You may buy it. But you may also like a wine from Australia or California; and sometimes you may be uncertain which to get. One thing that will help you decide is music. You will buy more French wine when you hear French music playing as you walk down the appropriate supermarket aisle. Really, it's true and innumerable tests have shown it to be so. Maybe you should put in earplugs as you go shopping.

The same principle is true of smells. Take bread. We want it to be fresh and we buy more when bread is baked "on the premises", and many stores have machines that pump out the smell of fresh-baked bread regardless of how far away in space and time the actual bakery may be; ditto freshly ground coffee. Even the characteristic smell of a new car will sometimes come from an aerosol.

I could go on. We buy more when a whole group of the same thing is displayed together, we are attracted to displays that move and buy more of the items in a supermarket that are displayed at eye level (higher for an average man than for a woman). Parents buy things to pacify or spoil children and shops exploit what is called "pester-power" by putting, say, confectionery where you wait at the checkout, just where a fractious child will have time to work its magic.

It's a minefield out there for the unwary shopper.

2. CONFUSION RULES

Ambiguity is the order of the day

"I know that you understand what you think I said,
but I am not sure you realize
that what you heard is not what I meant."
The late US President, Richard Nixon

SOMETIMES THINGS ARE NOT AS they seem. There is a story of a woman in a bookshop wanting to look at a book that was impossible to open because it was cellophane wrapped. "I suppose it's to keep them clean," she said to the assistant. "No, madam," came the reply."They are not wrapped to keep the dirt out, but to keep it in.". As we move on, we find things can most certainly confuse and they can do so in a variety of ways.

Let's start with some simple examples. Redcurrant jelly from Asda is labelled: *"NO FLAVOURS – We've done the hard work by removing each and every flavour from this product"*. Gosh, it must taste wonderful. This probably means something, though I'm not sure what – certainly it fails to make a positive point. The Gardener's Corner rain gauge measures rain in inches and millimetres and is evidently designed *"for indoor or outdoor use"*. Not only do they think it rains indoors, they put that first! Again, perhaps I'm missing something and it's actually a real selling point.

Every product provider wants to have good sales points and, above all, they want one winning one. This is what is known in marketing as a USP, or Unique Selling Proposition. This is not always easy to find when most products are so similar to so many others and winning description is made harder when what is written is at best as wobbly as Winnie the Pooh's spelling.

The Musical Heritage Society offers the music of Mozart on *"five fully digital CDs"*. I thought both that all CDs were digital and also that something was either digital or not; saying *"fully digital"* surely implies some things are only digital in part – which is in the same league as being a bit pregnant. Just a slip perhaps, but the trouble is that many people take technical terms to imply something good and throwing about words like digital and quantum can mislead. So the worthy society must join a number of others on the naughty step.

As an occasional asthma sufferer I am interested in anything that will help prevent or reduce it. AstraZeneca's Symbicot treatment is featured on the BioPortfolio web site where it says that asthma attacks can be *"fatal and recurrent"*. I know you can get repeated attacks. I know an attack can be dangerous or, at worst fatal, but surely if you got a fatal one at least you wouldn't get another; even if that's small comfort.

Baths are inevitably subject to some wear and tear. They can get scratched and spoiled, and because buying and fitting a new one is costly there are companies that will refurbish them for you. Various finishes are possible, but one odd one offered at www.refinishingonline.com is *"Anti Non Slip Bathtub & Shower Treatment"*. The real trouble here may be that it is actually somewhat difficult to refinish your bath online. Nevertheless, be very careful if you use that one; a great many accidents happen in bathrooms and I wouldn't be surprised if some were not fatal and recurrent.

A guard on a train departing from
London's Euston station announced:
Anyone found smoking will be extinguished

Haemorrhoids are a nasty affliction and best treated to get rid of them. The BMJ BestHealth web site offers a range of medical products and also says *"If you do not have an account and wish to purchase haemorrhoids click here"*. So if you have never had them and want to give them a try you can evidently buy some. As I say, you can, but me – well I have to say that it isn't on my list of 1000 things to experience before I die. I'll pass, thanks very much.

Even an apparently straightforward description can descend into difficulty. For example, the word fresh is surely clear enough; or is it? No doubt it varies depending on the product (and there has never seemed to me to be a need for a sell by date on sour cream), but what about this? A packet of UK butter from Marks and Spencer waxes lyrical about its contents: "*A smooth, creamy unsalted butter made with only the freshest summer milk from cows grazing on luscious summer pastures*". Sounds lovely, but summer milk? Bought in April this makes it at least eight months old. Fresh? It sounds like it is within a whisker of being sour cream. Just one word can make such a difference. An email from a health club says: "*Remember, you're a human being, not a human machine! Slow down. Make some time for yourself. You deserve it! Why not try a relaxing and distressing massage*". Other odd language and linguistic errors apart, "distressing" is definitely not the right word. Well I hope not.

Warnings of unwelcome ingredients abound and such is the state of worry about being sued that even the most inedible product's producer often feels it necessary to warn that it "may contain nuts". But what is one to make of a computer printer box warning that its contents "*may contain products from Switzerland*"? Okay Switzerland has its oddities and I have seen it described as the second most boring country in the world (there cannot, incidentally, be a *most* boring country as that would automatically make it interesting). But I have never seen it suggested before that things coming from Switzerland are dangerous, as this seems to imply. You never know though – better ditch that cuckoo clock quick.

Bottled water is, mystifyingly to me, a multi-million pound industry and many people really believe it is better for them than what comes out of the tap, never stopping to wonder why something billed as having taken four million years to trickle out of a glacier into its bottle has a sell-by date on the label. In deference to this, the words "designer water" have gone into the language; for some it is not enough to drink bottled water, it must be exclusive, expensive, posh bottled water. Maybe it *is* better than what comes out of the tap. Metromint demineralised water says on the label *"We start with pure water. We filter it for impurities so nothing gets in the way of it's* (sic) *clean crisp taste"*. Right, but if it was so pure to start with I wonder what it is that they filter out and what is left in it to give it its *"clean, crisp taste"*. Water is sent from one side of the world to the other in a liquid version of food miles and it is surely a waste of resources in most cases. Some of this is dictated by fashion. Fiji Water is served in London after a hugely long journey; justifying this a spokesman for the company said (to the *Guardian* newspaper) that soon *"... the production and sale of each bottle of water will actually result in a 120 per cent reduction of carbon in the atmosphere"*. No it won't, or is a major environmental disaster about to hit us?

> Sign in health food shop window:
> **Closed due to illness**

The science teacher at an English secondary school received goods ordered from a company called Scientific & Chemical Supplies. They arrived well packed in a box labelled *"Do not open"*. Ignoring this instruction, he found a further series of boxes inside all labelled the same way – a ploy to get you to order more, perhaps. This reminds me of supplies sent out by IT company, Equanet. On top of the box was printed in large letters *"I'm upside down. Please turn me over"*. On turning the box over, the same notice was revealed on the bottom. Maybe this is where the phrase about "never getting to the bottom of something" comes from.

Amazon is a supplier I love, but it is mentioned in these pages more than once. I regularly wonder about its recommendations: buy something – this book if you like – and they will tell what else you might like based on your choice. Sometimes (rarely?) these recommendations are sensible and useful, but buying, say, a cook book is just as likely to have you asked to consider a CD from some obnoxious pop singer or a camera, as to be recommended something else food related. I don't think that's because they think you might like music while you cook and to photograph the resultant dish, it is just wrong. Nevertheless they certainly sell a huge range of stuff and can both supply items themselves or put you in touch with other suppliers. This last can be a little disconcerting. One product, condoms, are listed as available *"used and new from £2.95"*.

Ikea is renowned for its flat pack furniture and there are those who say that you should buy nothing there unless you have a degree in reading between the lines of instructions and a great deal of spare time;, because of the way their shops operate it is difficult to be in and out quickly. It does not sell only furniture, of course, but its main business philosophy seems to have gone to its head: it sells light bulbs, some of which are in boxes adorned with their Allen key symbol and the words *"This product requires assembly"*. One wonders what else they think is required to assemble a light bulb beyond the Allen key – glass blowing equipment and a blast furnace? Perhaps they should have another label saying "Don't try this at home".

Sometimes things go wrong and we have to accept that. When this happens it is nice if those involved try to help. Even when they do, however, such well-intentioned advice may backfire. Parking in a local car park recently I saw that the ticket machine had a notice on saying *"Out of order. Please use other machine"*. Walking the length of the car park to the only other machine I found it had an identical notice on it. Perhaps more helpfully, the machines also had a notice on them saying, somewhat philosophically, *"Change is possible"*. Perhaps it forecast a change towards machines working at some point in the future or even a policy of allowing parking for free to protect a declining high street.

> A brochure inviting people to an event
> at a university states:
> **We have gone paperless.**
> Well, apart from the brochure presumably.

One sure sign that you should pause, take note and beware before buying is signalled by the word "new". Even the most basic claim can give pause for thought: on Jordan's cereal packet it says: *"The Original. New recipe with 10% more fruit"*. Sounds really different, doesn't it? Another word that you should regard as sounding alarm bells is "improved". Nothing seems to stay the same for five minutes, though changes may prove imperceptible, and this is true above all for computers, witness the short poem:

> *I bought a new computer,*
> *It came completely loaded.*
> *It was guaranteed for 90 days,*
> *But in 30 was outmoded.*

Of course things have to change. Some really need to change; like a recent mobile phone of mine which almost entirely failed to work in my own house unless I stood on a chair in one corner of the living room and faced south. Perhaps it was ever thus. I like a story told about one major innovation – the invention of the wheel. It is an oft-used phrase that we should "not keep reinventing the wheel", but just look a bit further back. This classic tale makes a good point:

> *The wheel was not invented in a flash of creative brilliance, like much else it initially had certain bugs and these took time to sort out. The very first wheels, the product of one of early man's first commercial enterprises the innovative Kwik-trip Korporation, were, in fact, square in shape. They did beat carrying heavy things, but only just – and it must be said that they gave a somewhat bumpy ride. Customers did buy them, well exchanged them as money hadn't been invented yet, but they also complained. Ug – the man who was in charge of new product development at KK- thought long and hard about possible changes. Then he had an idea.*
>
> *He set to work and made a new batch of wheels incorporating his new idea. When one of his best customers, arrived a few days later he proudly showed off his latest innovation. "A change for the better" said Ug, "it's new and improved" but his*

customer was not immediately enthusiastic "How on earth is that better?" he said "it's triangular!"

"That's right!" he was told enthusiastically "one less bump!"

Walker's crisps have a variant in
Worcester sauce flavour, the pack says:
NEW, IT'S BACK

I am old enough to believe that pubs are not what they once were. What's a gastro pub, for goodness sake? It seems like somewhere that, instead of serving you a nice steak pie, serves something "drizzled" onto your plate and charges you twice as much for half the food you expect. I have seen this sign in more than one pub: *"Children are not allowed in the pub or outside it"*. A catastrophic drop in population seems the inevitable consequence. Whether you go to the pub with children or not, you want to be safe and so you do at home too. One potential hazard in both places is fire, which takes me to my next example.

On the packaging for the First Alert smoke detector it says: *"Approximately 31 per cent of households have less than one working alarm. According to fire experts, this is not nearly enough"*. I think there is an important safety message in there somewhere, or maybe if more and more households have *"less than one"* fire alarm there will be more work for the fire service. Anyway, it seems to me that it would be more powerful to say not "less than one" but none.

Albert Einstein is reputed to have told someone "If we knew what it was we were doing, it would not be called research, would it?" That apart, I am greatly in favour of companies finding out what customers think of their products and service. One easy way to do this is to put a questionnaire in with the product for customers to complete and return once the product is in use. Morphy Richards do this with their Turbojet steam iron and, along with questions about its performance, ask people *"Which factor most influenced your decision to buy a new appliance?"* Amongst the options to tick, such as *"Setting up home"*, is: *"Wanting to eat more healthily"*. Irons are pretty sophisticated these days, but I didn't think they had much to do with food preparation. Most such questionnaires are as much about getting information about you as about your feelings about the product; some offer you an incentive such as putting your name in a draw, and all ask for contact information that will enable them to bombard you with sales messages in every form possible.

There is a great tendency to indiscriminately throw good sounding words into product descriptions in an attempt to make them sound more attractive – even if what is being said is, well, somewhat contrived or inappropriate. I am sure that Ampleforth Abbey is jolly good cider but describing it as *"Made from biologically grown apples*" rather misses the mark – though if they used any apples that were *not* biologically grown that might indeed be news. Worse is this example where the word infinite is dropped in: a double glazing leaflet promises to "*... make your home infinitely warmer and safer*". Infinitely warmer would surely be hell and thus more than hot enough to be anything but safe.

Label: **Blackcurrant juice comes in two flavours – orange and strawberry**

Craftmatic make adjustable beds. The idea is that they deliver an exceptional level of comfort, something that is especially important if you have a bad back. For anyone so afflicted and thinking of buying a new bed, what are you to make of this description telling you that Craftmatic provides "*a lifetime of temporary relief*" for chronic back pain. I would want that word temporary somewhat more closely defined, and certainly for it to be describing something that lasts for more than a couple of seconds.

On a map of walking routes in Cornwall,
one route is labelled
Non-existent footpath

An office sign warns *"No smoking alarms in use"*. Maybe they prosecute if you do smoke and sound an alarm if you don't. In a similar vein, in one hotel in Hawaii another notice says *"No smoking prohibited by law"* so maybe clamping down on people who don't smoke is spreading. Allowing confusion about things that might get you fined is bad enough, but smoking can also provoke arguments: "You can't smoke here" says the aggrieved non-smoker; "Yes I can" says the smoker, "It says that *not* smoking here is prohibited". This sort of thing could lead rapidly to Accident & Emergency.

Seriously... be warned

When you read something intended to inform and do a sort of double take, wondering if you quite understand, pause and think it through. A lack of precision in one area may indicate an uncaring attitude in others. If a company cannot even be bothered to check what it says on its labels, or worse wants them to confuse, what else may they be bad at? If production control is bad, then the product may not work. If customer service is bad you may not be able to exchange it, at least in a straightforward manner, and if safety factors are not thoroughly checked the product may be dangerous (witness the surprisingly large number of product recalls you read about in the press every year).

Maybe you do not want to buy stuff from a

company that is vague, convoluted or hooked on gobbledegook. If so, then seeing that Morrison's toilet cleaner claims that it *"cleans, freshens and kills germs"* might make you want to pick another brand: one that just kills them outright. It seems to me that to freshen them up and perhaps give them a false sense of hope and security before they get the chop is rather cruel.

INTERLUDE

Increasing desperation

Most products will have competition – and will be very like their competitors. Then the supplier has to somehow describe it to boost its attractiveness. First off they may describe everything about it, such as with this fictitious FINE product:

"SPLODGE – the big, wholesome, tasty, non-fattening, instant, easily prepared, chocolate pudding for the whole family"

Or one factor could be stressed, thus implying that competitive products are lacking in this respect:

"SPLODGE – the easily prepared pudding"

Customers may know all such puddings are easy to prepare, but they hope you will conclude this is easiest. But in a crowded market there are probably puddings being advertised already as "easily prepared", and big, wholesome and all the rest for that matter. What then? Well one way out is to pick another factor ignored by competitors because it is not essential:

"SPLODGE – the pudding in the ring pull pack"

This may be a marginal factor but the advertisement now implies it's important and that competition is lacking. Alternatively a characteristic of total irrelevance is featured:

"SPLODGE – the pudding that floats in water"

If competition has done all of this then there is only one alternative, to feature something else, nothing to do with the product. This may necessitate giving something away:

"SPLODGE – the only pudding sold with a *free* sink plunger"

Or re-package:

"SPLODGE – the only pudding in the *transparent* ring pull pack"

The possibilities are endless and the ultimate goal is always to make a product appear different and attractive, and desirable because of it.

Additionally, advertising has to be made to look attractive. Sometimes this may be achieved through added humour, personalities and whatever, or through lavish production values – some television commercials (from big brands) clearly cost far more per minute than the programmes they punctuate. As ever the moral is to be wary.

Note: this is adapted from my book Marketing *available on line from www.quicklookbooks.com*

3. NO WAY

Believing any number of impossible things

"If you can't convince them, confuse them."

Harry Truman

IN THE BRAVE NEW WORLD of consumerism there are many promises made. There are products that we are told will change our diet, our house or our whole life, but perhaps it is worth treating all such claims with caution; sometimes with extreme caution. Take travel: however good a holiday you have booked, there is first the small matter of getting there. Travel any distance overseas and this will inevitably involve a flight. Ignoring, for the moment, the hassle and tedium that combine to create the horror of the airport experience, what about the plane? The airlines are always at pains to tell us how wonderful the experience of flying is. Flight announcements as you take off always end with the words, *"Enjoy your flight"*, and though some airlines have the good grace to say that they *"hope"* you enjoy it, so many things conspire to render this about as likely as winning the lottery that the words never ring true. After all how can several hours crushed in a tiny seat inside a metal tube, being dehydrated, watching a cut-down version of a film of which the best review said "dire" and eating dinner at breakfast time next to a fat, flatulent fidget be in any small way pleasurable? Hong Kong, America, Thailand, Peru, and much of the rest of the world may be fun when you get there, but finding the journey pleasurable is well-nigh impossible.

The British Airports Authority web site tells you, if you look up the page about London's Heathrow airport, which has been well described in the press as a national embarrassment, that *"you'll find everything here to make your journey through the airport easy and enjoyable"*. Well from bitter personal experience I can tell you that easy and enjoyable – It. Will. Not. Be. You are more likely to find eating the entire contents of your hand luggage and washing it down with sulphuric acid enjoyable. In fact you may well need to do that to get the weight of it down to many an airline's measly allowance. The whole experience is... enough, I will resist digressing into details of airport and flight experiences I would rather forget and concentrate on other impossibilities.

Ladders must be used at all times
says a notice in a garage. What, even when sweeping
the floor? How do you do that?

Alice was faced with impossible things when she went through the looking glass. She told the White Queen that she could not believe in impossible things. The Queen replies: "I dare say you haven't had much practice. When I was your age, I always did it for half-an-hour a day. Why, sometimes I've believed as many as six impossible things before breakfast." Here we look at the many impossible things put to us by suppliers. They want us to believe impossible things, do impossible things and regard impossible things as good reasons to give them our business.

First, and there are dozens of versions of this, there is something that seems to be a stock in trade of the software industry. Obsessive about their gubbins being used correctly, their packs say things like *"Do not open until you have read and understood the enclosed end user license agreement"*. I can't do that, I won't do that and it puts me off the whole idea of even looking at the wretched agreement, much less abiding by it. How many people ever actually read this sort of thing, I wonder; I suspect it's vanishingly few. The same is true of terms and conditions. If I had a pound for every person who has clicked the "I have read and accept the terms and conditions" box online without a glance at the detail I would be a millionaire.

A computer message appearing while using Adobe Photoshop says: **The Adobe Updater must update itself before it can check for updates. Would you like to update Adobe Updater now?** By the sound of this, even if you do want to, it's impossible.

The web site at University College London asks students logging in to *"make sure that your new password is between 7 and 8 characters"*. That's impossible I think, unless they have students there studying mathematics and versed in something like imaginary numbers who know better. Let's hope it was not someone from the Department of Mathematics who set that up. Also to do with computers: at Sydney airport security tells passengers *"Laptop computers are to be removed from cases and presented in two separate pieces at the X-ray machine"*. Well I hope that's impossible, it would certainly break mine, though with some models you can click off the keyboard to make a tablet.

Cooking can be difficult and even barbecuing, which many a man claims to be able to do, can present problems. The M & M "Fall-off-the-bone" frozen ribs packet tells purchasers to: *"Place thawed ribs on grill and heat for 10 minutes. Turn halfway through and continue grilling until thoroughly heated. To avoid burning, keep bone side of ribs facing down for two-thirds of the heating time."* Either that is impossible or I don't understand it, or both. But it's more likely than the lamb joints sold by Sainsbury's that tell you to cook them at 1900 degrees C. No normal oven would do that and getting that kind of detail wrong could conceivably lead to downright dangerous situations, as someone sets up a blast furnace to try and comply. The population on the naughty step is growing.

Remember that all the text quoted here is designed to help a product stand out from competition and prompt you to buy it, rather than a competitive product. Sometimes perhaps the urge to do this goes too far. A bottle of bleach says it *"Kills bacteria as well as the leading competition"*. Surely it can't do that and, in any case, create a monopoly like that and someone might just notice. Another cleaning product, Jeyes Parazone Anti-Limescale Block, claims: *"Stops Limescale FOREVER"*, now that's an awfully long time and I would suggest this is impossible. Actually it does add *"with continuous use"*, which removes the impossibility but makes the claim seem a bit pedestrian. Still, I suppose they have to try to make it sound special.

A card handed out to departing passengers at Sydney airport read: **Has anyone put anything in your luggage without your knowledge?** An impossible question to answer surely and one to which one can only respond with a "Don't know".

Maybe translation makes absurdities more likely. One wonders about this one as Seat cars are made in Spain. The manual for the Alhambra describes a *"Park Assist feature that enables the Alhambra to park itself – just like magic"*. Wow, sounds impressive, but in fact it's not like magic at all as it goes on to say *"Requires driver control"*. Harry Potter can relax. They have added that in after an asterisk, so I suspect it is not translation causing the problem, it's just that in their excitement they can't resist talking up each and every feature to make it sound great even if ultimately the magic palls. So for the moment the phrase *"park itself"* needs to be translated to say that actually the driver must park the car but this model does offer a little electronic assistance.

There are no translation problems as far as I know with this next one. Boots own brand of Multivitamins for Men has a warning *"During pregnancy and lactation or if you are trying to get pregnant we suggest you consult your doctor or pharmacist before taking this product"*. First off, Boots, you should know that it's impossible for men to get pregnant; they just don't – not even a little bit. Second off, anything like this needs instructions that are as clear as crystal. One is left wondering if the person who wrote this is brain dead or if actually they are trying to say that it could affect a man's ability to make someone pregnant, in which case some real explanation is surely necessary. I also liked another item about vitamins which said that *"people with a vitamin D deficiency are as much as twice as likely to die compared to people whose blood contains higher amounts..."*. Literally, this means that you are half as likely to die if you do the business with vitamin D. Not only is that impossible but most of us accept, however reluctantly, that the likelihood of death is actually 100%.

Computer pop up:

Cannot delete file. There is not enough free disc space. Delete one or more files to free disk space, and then try again.

Don't you just *love* computers!?

In a school where the playground completely surrounds the buildings there is a sign saying: *"Deliveries: All deliveries must report to reception BEFORE entering the playground"*. That would be a trick the children should see. Also appertaining to transportation was the announcement on London Underground that *"There are no trains travelling in both directions between Victoria and Brixton"*. Right – not now, not ever there aren't; at least without some radical alteration of the laws of physics.

Train travel seems to be full of such impossibilities almost as regularly as engineering works stop you travelling anywhere on a Sunday. Sometimes they get truly odd. A London Underground station announcement at Holborn once said: "*As you enter the platform please move left and right away from the entrances*". At the same station another impossible request was heard: "*Please use both sides of the escalators – standing on the left and walking on the right*". This is the same station that once posted a notice saying that "*Camden Town station is closed due to a localised event taking place*", perceptively making it clear that whatever it was causing the problem, it was not world-wide. Greater precision was heard in an announcement at King's Cross station "*The next train will be at the platform in approximately a few minutes*"; no likelihood of missing that then.

Sign in hospital lift:
The fourth floor has moved to the ninth floor.
If that's not impossible then I hope they did it carefully or the whole building might now be unstable.

Maybe we need to consult a modern day Einstein about this one. Some items sold by Orvis, who make up-market clothes for men and women (that's making some clothes for each sex), are made in a fabric described as "*4-way stretch*". Not in this universe they aren't. But wait a moment, maybe they are not in this universe: another label describes something made of

"*2.5 layers*", which seems a pretty outlandish kind of cloth – other worldly, perhaps.

You can buy Orvis clothes mail order, but I'm not sure how they dispatch them. If they use Royal Mail then they might like to know that the Post Office offers a track and trace service so that you can monitor the progress of something en route to its destination. All being well, if you log onto the appropriate website and put in your tracking number you get a notice saying "*Recorded Signed For*" with capital letters suggesting firmly that whatever it is you sent has arrived. Uncertainty may come to mind when you read on: "*... items are only tracked after the item has been delivered. Depending on whether the item was sent first or second class, this may be a few days after posting. Please try again later.*" If I understand this correctly, it's actually impossible to track things at all, though you can find out that they have arrived once they have done so, but their arrival may take some time. If you are trying to track something being sent to you then the easiest thing to do is just wait until it arrives, because if it does not do so then they won't be able to tell you anything anyway. My response to this is in danger of getting as convoluted as the official note, so I'll move on.

In a hospital corridor, a hamper for used bed sheets is labelled: **Empty when half full.** No, that's impossible; it's empty when there is nothing at all in it.

Now for something that seems to be believable. Good, reliable old Microsoft again flashing messages to me as I work. One said *"There is not enough memory to complete the..."*. Not true, incidentally. I forget what I was doing at the time, but having cancelled the message the task did complete.

There are so many of these statements and this next case relates to the way the product works. Scotts Of Stow offer a compass saying *"This ingeniously designed compass is far easier to read, as it always points in the direction you are heading"*. No, that's impossible – it points north or it would not be a compass, and anyway we usually know which way we are heading – but we may want to know where north is. It's all rather confusing. Maybe if it is so special you could use it indoors, where in one office building there is a sign in the lift saying *"Only use the buttons provided"*. I know some people who are frightened of using lifts, but they do not, to the best of my knowledge, take their own, more trustworthy, buttons with them.

If all this relentless impossibility is getting you down, cheer up and have some chocolate. Many people try to ration their consumption of this fattening substance, but if you want to share a little treat then you should avoid Feodora "Mint for two". This product appears to suggest keeping your consumption down through an amicable division of just half each. Even if you think this is a neat idea you cannot do so – the contents are "*13 mini-mints*". The mints are small, by the sound of it, but the odd number will likely to lead to major arguments.

Keeping up to date with making sure that all the many gadgets in your life have functioning batteries may sometimes seem like a full time job. You need to keep an eye on them and some, like watches, stop working with little or no warning of the batteries' demise. The Bush portable DVD player is different, the instructions say "*When the battery pack is fully charged, the battery pack charge indicator will turn green*". That seems clear enough until you read on: "*Note: Because of the characteristics of lithium-ion batteries, when the battery pack charge indicator turns green it does not mean the battery pack is fully charged*". So you now know why DVDs have a tendency to grind to halt just when the hero is about to get the chop – what will happen? Does he survive? The green light will evidently not help to provide the answer.

Sometimes you will see things that are possible and sometimes you will see things that are impossible. Sometimes the wording is so convoluted that the truth of the matter is just not clear and you are not sure what is impossible and what is not. If in doubt you need Dettox Anti-Bacterial Cleanser, the label on which proclaims it *"wipes away doubt"*. There you are then, now we can move on to the next chapter and think about time.

Seriously... be warned

The Weapons of Mass Disinformation strike again.

It can be frustrating just as you are forming a view of a product to be faced with a seeming impossibility, especially if, on balance, you were pretty much decided to buy. Again, such nonsense may give you pause for thought. You will certainly have to read between the lines, as it were, and decide whether the people posing you the quandary are to be trusted to give you the value for money you want.

Remember that brand names are designed to act like a guarantee: it is intended that if you buy the one with the name you know and the image you like then you will not find yourself disappointed. When the image cracks, then so does the promise.

INTERLUDE

Bearing gifts

The ultimate free gift was probably the Trojan Horse and that turned out to be full of soldiers and thus did the Greeks no good at all. Products often come with free gifts too and sometimes their worth is easy to assess. A toothbrush with a free tube of toothpaste or vice versa may be compared with other offerings and may indeed be a bargain; perhaps it is less costly than the two items bought separately. This is only true, however, if you actually want whatever extra is added; you may waste money if the free gift ends up buried in some cupboard or thrown away because you hate the taste or whatever. So some care is necessary. One part of your brain is saying *free! Free! FREE!* and wanting to buy regardless of anything else, while another part is trying to assess whether the deal is really worthwhile.

A bit of a trick in this area is the so called self-liquidating offer. Here you do pay for something, but it is described as a bargain and it is only available when you buy the main product. Be aware of how this works: imagine that the deal is a camera. You buy something and get a camera for a discounted price: "Worth £40.00, you pay only £10.00 – save £30.00!". Here the manufacturer has found a source of cheap cameras and is paying only say £5.00 each for them, so actually they make a profit every time you "save money". Much that is offered in this way proves not to be the "good deal" it seems. So next time you buy a chocolate mousse and a free sink plunger comes with it, make sure that you actually want the sink plunger. You could end up with an overpriced dessert and have three or four sink plungers in your kitchen cupboard gathering dust.

4. CHEAP AT HALF THE PRICE

Price, discounts and value for money

*"People want economy and they will
pay any price to get it."*

Lee Iacocca

SOMEONE IS AFTER YOUR HARD earned money. Actually lots of people are after it. This is the one clear, overriding reason for companies to communicate with us: they want our money. They will go to quite some lengths to get it too; those with something to sell can be, well, on occasion the word pushy doesn't really cover it. An apocryphal tale makes this clear – there was once a salesman who managed to sell a farmer with one cow two milking machines – and who then financed the deal by taking the cow as a down payment!

With money in mind there is one big, overall, inherent clash between consumers and suppliers. Consumers want a bargain, or at the very least we want value for money, and suppliers want to make as much money from their customers as possible. There is one seeming contradiction with this: sometimes we actually *want* to spend more. No, you say I don't; well I beg to differ – sometimes you do. No one buys a Rolls Royce because it's cheap – it's very much not – and the same could be said for a wide range of luxury goods. I discovered only recently that, despite mobile phones coming with a near infinite selection of ring tones, some people choose to pay additional money for a different one. I barely believed it, but it's true, and proves without question that some people have money to burn. Sometimes products are actually promoted as costing a lot: Stella Artois beer is sold with the slogan *"Reassuringly expensive"* and it sells very well. We like posh products, we like exclusivity and we like to spoil ourselves. But we also like a bargain and Stella no doubt sells even better when it's on special offer.

So here we look at price, at saving money and at our overall aim of getting value for money. Let's start with this: every second advertisement on television seems to aim to sell you insurance and many of these are put out by the comparison sites. One of these seems a bit confused about value for money. It mentions savings and specifically a sum of £137.43, then saying: *"The money you can claw back on household insurance is invaluable"*. So it's worth a mint then or, wait a minute, isn't it actually worth just £137.43? You know that and so do I. The company believing otherwise is, appropriately enough, called Confused.com.

A flyer from Domino Pizza says:
Savings up to and over £220.00.
It just makes you wonder how much they were
in the first place.

Sometimes companies waste money rather than make it. I had a row with Orange about my non-operating broadband. It took them some three months to fix it, a period made worse by the fact of their apparently brain dead customer service staff sending me emails and my having to patiently explain at length over the phone: no broadband = no emails. They gave me a dongle as part of settling up with me (and some compensation – the moral is persistence and well written letters) but when used that clocked up a bill of more than £50.00 and failed to connect me to anything. They waived the bill and, although I have not used the wretched thing since, they send me regular bills demanding £0.00. Then the debt changed to "£0.01" and they sent endless reminders of this huge debt at a cost of... I know not what. Dare I hope that they will read this and stop completely? I won't hold my breath – but I digress. The point is that everyone wants to make money from us and the relentless pursuit of just a single penny shows how deeply felt this need is.

Back to value for money: however carefully you think you buy, I am afraid that getting the best deal, or even getting a good deal, may be difficult if not well-nigh impossible. Even trying can be a complex process.

Consider mobile phones. Most people check around, balancing the way they use their phone in terms of calls, texts, email and these days also games, music and more to get a good deal. Top of the list on a search I made on the Internet was Moneysupermarket.com offering to help me compare *"more than 800,000"* tariffs. There are, almost unbelievably, 800,000 different ways of signing up to be able to say "I'm on the train". It's nice to have a choice, but isn't this just the tiniest bit over the top? It's surely choice gone mad and is, in any case, utterly unmanageable.

Actually it's an example of what marketers call *confusion pricing*. The providers *want* choosing to be complicated. If it is difficult to make real comparisons then their superficial blandishments are more likely to get frustrated consumers rejecting the whole comparison business as impossible – or at least impossibly time consuming – and opting for what they hope is a good deal by taking a superficial glance at the details or just picking what they hope is the best of a confusing bunch. Numbers of suppliers use confusion pricing, as you will know if you have gone anywhere recently by train, tried to work out which company to buy gas from or asked about travel insurance. Incidentally most insurance comparison sites bring a whole new meaning to the old idea of comparing apples with apples as they are more like comparing apples with old boots.

While on the subject of insurance, I recently got a quote from Norwich Union to insure my car. Not unreasonably they wanted to know where it was kept and none of the options given seemed to fit – not on the road, not in a garage – so I telephoned them, well their man in Bombay, and, agreeing that none did fit, he put it down as *"don't know"*. How can that possibly be an answer to the question *"Where do you habitually keep your car overnight?"* How can anyone, even a habitual drunk, not know where they usually put the car as they go to bed? This alone put me off signing up with them and so, as a test, I telephoned their claim line – how an insurer deals with an accident is after all what matters most. And they... no, I won't bore you with the details, but I went elsewhere. On a brighter note, I notice that as the economics changes a number of overseas call centres (or what those in the business prefer to be known as contact centres) are being repatriated to home soil. Even the bank Santander, who the newspapers always seem to list at being worse with complaints than anyone else, are ditching Mumbai for some northern city. A good sign I hope.

So back to price: price and value is an area about which the wily purchaser needs to have all their wits about them. Buy and use a calculator, but don't pay too much for it. Thinking of mobile phones again, it is wise to watch out for another word much used to hook customers and get them to buy: that is "upgrade". Upgrade sounds good, better and desirable. Sign up for a mobile with the promise of an upgrade at the end of your contract and you will have something to look forward to. It means a better phone, unlimited texts, a lower tariff or more. Perhaps it also means a shorter contract, better roaming facilities and a red rose delivered on your birthday. Think so? Think again. It is more likely to mean paying out more money, having to sign up for a longer period and getting a phone which only the least technically sophisticated person on the planet would regard as in any small way "better". Be warned, read the small print or, to be really economic, just get two tin cans and tie them together with string... and whatever you do, please don't shout mindless blather into your phone all the way to London when you are sitting opposite me on the train. I don't want to know about last night's curry, how you nailed young Tracy from Accounts or the size of your hangover; upgrade to silence.

A sign at a multi-story car park says there will be a charge of £15.00 for **"releasing cars outside opening hours"**. Alongside it says: **Open 24 hours**

At least you know that "two for the price of one" is saving you money. Or do you? Tesco once had a shelf label stating that cartons of soup were £1.00 or "*Any two for £3.00*". And how about the bookshop that was seen offering "*Fantasy fiction – 2 for the price of 3*"? It may be fantasy but it's also fantastically expensive fantasy. Before we go into special offers, remember that confusion pricing is just one of many dubious tactics used to get consumers to cough up hard earned cash. It is worth knowing about such tactics. So pay attention, these include:

- *Drip pricing:* consisting of a low headline price that expands as you investigate it. This is something certain budget airlines excel in; some say they invented it. Sometimes the actual cost of a full fare is 20 times that shown up front. How long will it be before they charge extra if you wear a coat? (Incidentally, I recently read that you can now buy a "budget airline coat" with enormous strong pockets, including a laptop-sized one, so that half the weight you want to carry can go about your person to combat obscene baggage costs). And why don't they apply this policy to something that will help passengers? I would love to hear them say *Sorry, Mrs Wellington, but little Wayne is making too much noise, it will cost you an extra £1000.00 or he will have to go in the hold.* Go on Ryanair, do it: and make the cost so high that parents just have to opt for the hold and others get a quieter flight. You can tell I've had more than one flight ruined by rambunctious ankle biters; usually wholly unchecked by their parents.

- *Bait pricing:* this is when one enormous reduction on a single item is used to attract people to a sale where other reductions are not in the same league.

- *Reference pricing:* here a special price is compared with the apparent norm: "Usually £220, now only £99" screams the banner. It usually means that a branch of the shop located in the Hebrides had it on show, though it was visible only in the basement. At the back. Hidden behind a filing cabinet. For 20 minutes... after the branch had closed. Ok, yes, maybe I do exaggerate – but only a bit.

- *Time-limited offers:* only available today, this week, during February they say, hoping this will prompt a quick and perhaps irrational decision to buy right now – but the offer is still there in six months.

- *Free offers:* that just are not. I got awarded a free holiday recently and when the details arrived it was £140 odd pounds – provided I took it within the next two weeks! Any later and the cost went up. And to think I spent a moment being excited about it; I should know better.

Even a phrase like "free delivery" can be misused. A specialist clothes retailer's catalogue tells customers *"You can pick up your order from any one of our Rohan shops and delivery will be free"*. But that's not actually free delivery at all, it's called collection and so I should jolly well think it would be free. Be careful at sales: making a saving or getting a bargain is always satisfying, but beware how uncritically you aim for a saving. One *bait pricing* trap again involves the words "up to". *"Savings of up to 60%"* on a sign outside a furniture shop for instance, may be good news, but equally it could mean that the only item at a 60% discount is a single shop soiled sofa with cushions that would only match day old sick.

There are regulations about the sorts of thing listed above and there need to be more. Watch out: a whole host of offers are not what they seem, and sometimes dramatically so. Research by Mysupermarket.co.uk recently listed: Tesco charging £2.00 more for a pack of 12 Pepsis than the total cost of two packs of six; Asda selling eight Gillette razor blades for £14.91,when a packet of four was £5.00; and Sainsbury's pricing a 800g jar of Hellman's mayonnaise at £2.99, with a 400g jar of the same stuff at £1.00. Can these people just not work with numbers or might such things be because so many of us grab unthinkingly at special offers? On another occasion Tesco offered Options instant Belgian drinking chocolate at 23p adding that if you bought before 3 January 2010 you could get four for £1.00. It was not better to wait for that, then. If you are saying to yourself, "I would never fall for that", think again – we are all gullible, or inattentive, to a degree. A profusion of surveys over many years has shown that we all buy more when prices just miss a round figure. Prices set at 99p, £9.99 and even £9,999 all get more people saying yes than the same thing at £10.00 and so on. Why? Because psychologically we love a bargain and in a sense we allow ourselves to be fooled; it is the same thinking that has people emerging from the summer sales saying "I saved over £100!" No, not so – you *spent* £200.

Catalogue entry:

Scandinavian slippers – buy one get one free

All this is actually serious stuff and the moral is to pause, think, check and not be fooled. You may spend less as a result. And we all want to pay less. Air New Zealand promote round the world trips *"from £698 return"*. Ignoring the "from" ploy for a moment (which with airlines tends to mean that to get the fare advertised you have book 18 months in advance and fly on a Thursday when there is a R in the month), does this mean that a one-way round trip only costs £349? Sadly, I am sure the answer was no, though last time I checked going "round the world" does bring you back to where you started.

Buying something can certainly give you pleasure. But however carefully you buy, bills seem to have a habit of catching up with you. One customer of telecom giant BT received an email telling him he owed on his business broadband account £87.51000000 00000005. Despite this nonsense figure they added that failure to pay promptly *"could lead to a late payment charge of £10.00"*. In isolation £10.00 may not be so much, unless it's £10.00 more than you expect. T-Mobile advertises *"Free internet and texts for life"*, but curiously only if you pay £10.00 each month. Similarly an article about the Freesat television system explained, all in one breath as it were, that *"There's no subscription and no monthly bills to pay. Prices start from as little as £2.99 per month"*. They should really understand the meaning of the word "free"; it's in their name after all. Meanwhile over in Canada, Direct Energy offers: *"Special free offer! Free maintenance – only $13.99 a month"*.

In a Dublin (of course) shop, the sign:
Everything under 5 euro – or less

If you are finding it difficult to work out what some of this means, then sometimes helpful comparisons are offered: in Asda frozen spinach is priced at 89p for a one kilogram pack, with a notice alongside that says this is *"£89.00 per 100 kilograms"*. So you don't need that calculator after all; and that's so helpful to anyone who can even imagine what 100 kilograms of spinach looks like. It would keep Popeye up to strength for months. Even more mystifying, Superdrug sell a toothbrush for £1.44. Sounds like a fair price and if you are not sure they tell you that is equivalent to *"£7.58 per metre"*. Oops. Similarly helpful information is provided by Tesco which sells fitness three-kilogram hand weights for £3.99 which is, the label says, *"£1.33 per kilogram"*. Perhaps the more you spend the fitter you get and with this information you can presumably easily weigh up (sorry!) how many to buy.

Every parent knows the agony of buying some gadget or toy for Christmas and then finding that their child can't play with it without batteries and spends the rest of the festive day fractious and in tears. So it is encouraging to see the Early Learning Centre's toy catalogue offering items *"With batteries free of charge"*. No tears at Christmas there then, but, wait a minute. If they are free of charge then surely they won't power the toy. Back to square one. A Google search produced another freebie: *"Free CDs. Huge selection of free CDs in stock at discount prices"*.

Other things may be free too and you would expect a bank to be able to present this clearly. But Barclays gave one customer a quotation for a mortgage that said *"No early repayment charges are applied to this mortgage. However, a final repayment charge which is currently £275.00 is payable if you repay your mortgage in full before the end of the mortgage term"*. So it seems that the charge you don't pay for repaying early amounts to £275.00. That's a good bit more than the nothing they firmly state it will be in the first sentence. With that level of precision calculation, no wonder the banks failed and had to be bailed out by the government.

Actually banks have trouble with other matters too. ING ask you, reasonably enough, to complete a form to open an online savings account, but it asks you to indicate whether you are "male" "female" or "unknown". Does that mean there is a category for people who don't know what gender they are or is it for those who live a solitary existence and who nobody knows? It can't be the latter because if you open a savings account then however much of a hermit you are the bank knows you thereafter. Lloyds TSB are not that numerate either, promoting their insurance by saying *"On average our customers found they saved up to £98 by switching to us"*. Maybe they will give me an overdraft which can be on average up to £500. Then if one day one I run it up to a million quid, I can hope it will take them a while to calculate an average. Averages are funny things. On an average speed check road, I have heard it said that you can perfectly legally stop early on for a smoke and then drive through the rest at 90 mph. Probably best not to try this on the M25, though.

Sign at car dealership:

Up to £3000 minimum trade in

So free things are not always free, in which case finding a lower price is the best way to go. Wal-Mart is obviously the best place to shop for everything as they offer *"Lower prices every day"*. The only question is how much they will reduce by each day and how soon everything will be free. If it is not going to be too long, form a queue now.

Mostly suppliers are communicating with numbers of people, often large numbers of people, for mass market products and services. Sometimes, though, something is offered just for a single person. Easyjet is an example: *"Be first to board your flight for just £7.50 per person"*. Sounds very exclusive, unless they sell this deal to more than one person; if you buy this and do not board alone, demand your money back. For some suppliers, just making the offer of savings, discounts or special deals is not enough. They can't just say "30% off", they throw in other words, like HomeSense, whose store in Reading promised *"unique home wear always up to 60% less*", though what makes a bog standard product unique is unexplained and so is what it is always less than. Or the notice of a kitchen sale that said *"up to a genuine 35% off"*. This seems to presuppose that lots of sales are not genuine. Or do they mean that all 35% s are not the same; if so, perhaps they should have paid more for their calculator. Some deals are assuredly not what they seem, so I guess it's nice if even suppliers warn us of this.

A Boots store was seen offering:
3 for 2 flight socks.
For that difficult third foot.

An added complication to assessing value for money is Value Added Tax, which is currently at 20% in the United Kingdom. On an item of any real price, this can significantly up the cost and you have to watch to see if prices include it or not. Photobox makes a charge of £8.50212765957447 for 250 megabytes of online storage, but this does not include VAT which at the time this was flagged brought it up to a neat £9.99. It's almost a relief to be paying the tax just to get a straightforward figure. How would anyone give change for £8.50212765957447? Luckily this was offered online; I would hate to be next in the queue behind someone sorting out that sort of quandary at a cashpoint.

Even if you spend nothing there is money to be saved. Scottish Power sensibly suggest *"Common sense ways to save energy"*, offering as one idea that customers should *"Switch your TV, hi-fi or video off at the mains and you'll save 60 per cent of the energy it uses on standby mode"*. 60% is it? Actually it's better than that: if you switch it off at the mains you actually save 100% of the power it would otherwise use. Yes, really Scottish Power, all of it. So then it costs nothing. But wait a minute – in that case your TV will develop two small faults: no sound and no picture.

Other savings are clearly stated but hardly cost effective. On line retailer Amazon have the following offer: "Product Promotions. Save £0.02 when you spend £100,000.00 or more on Qualifying Items offered by Amazon.co.uk". Oh joy! Irresistible. The problem will be how to decide what to spend that great saving on. Amazon also sells Sanyo rechargeable batteries at £16.27 for four. This they add (proudly?) represents a saving of £3,560,000.00 and that saving is "100 per cent". A complete lack of any number sense pervades that offer, also the one offering savings on computer printer ink of "... between 30 – 300 per cent". Presumably at the higher level they must pay you to take it away. Now that would be a good deal, but I bet any savings are at the lower end of the scale. As an example of spanning the total range of possibilities without even the tiniest degree of clarity, I offer you online clothing retailer Land's End whose clearance sale offered savings of "up to 50 per cent or more". That range of price is literally unimaginable, but it could still include items with only a few pence off and have such a saving match the headline. That sort of thing is just plain wrong and too often one suspects that it is just piling on words, however illogical, to try to make an offer sound good.

Okay, grudgingly I accept that in the computer age bizarre calculations may be made inadvertently and missed; just one mistaken click is all it takes. But I cannot really see why the Australia and New Zealand Bank print all the paying in slips used in their branches with boxes for customers to enter the sum paid in and put 10 boxes on them. How many people pay in sums up towards a thousand million over the counter – even in Australian dollars? Let's be generous, perhaps they just don't want to keep the odd guy who arrives with a fork lift truck full of cash waiting while they organise a special form.

Seriously ... be warned

So, let me repeat: if something seems too good to be true pricewise, then it usually is. If it says "free" then it may well not be and if a price is hedged around with complex descriptions, percentages, discounts and the like, you need to be careful. Check. Then use your calculator, and check again. For everyone who says "I've got a bargain!" there are several more who find they have been confused, misled or, at worst, signed up to pay an escalating monthly sum for the next 10 years on a product that will be obsolete in two.

INTERLUDE

Them and us

Another way that you are targeted to buy involves testimonials. Now, make no mistake, some testimonials are invaluable and they are certainly different in nature to a company just saying – *We think it's great. Buy it.* If, for example, you are buying a new car and checking it out carefully, which is most credible: is it, i) the car salesman (it is nearly always a man) saying "This model will do 55 miles per gallon" , or ii) when you are told "An independent test in *What car?* Magazine showed that this model will do 55 mph"? No contest; for almost all of us it's the latter – the testimonial. In this example the testimonial comes from a magazine, but often in advertising it comes from an individual.

Various well-known sportsmen endorse razor blades. Film stars endorse cosmetics or, in the case of James Bond, watches. Michael Parkinson is used to sell insurance and Disney characters and the like are used to sell cereal and other products (many aimed at children). Successful films are linked to everything from hamburgers to computer games.

This technique is just everywhere. For goodness sake, actress Dawn French helps advertise chocolate, even though she is hardly a role model for those wanting to avoid fattening food. And, make no mistake, it all works; we buy more. Even a well-known, recognisable personality as the voice over on a commercial may be sufficient to add a note of respectability and reassurance to whatever is being sold.

Always remember that such people are *paid* to do this and often paid a great deal of money. I am sure Daniel Craig is very happy with his Omega watch, but do not make the mistake of thinking that such people are volunteering to do this only because they think the product is so good. It's another ploy to make you buy more.

5. IGNORE THE INSTRUCTIONS AT YOUR PERIL

The bizarre dos and don'ts of product use

*"The customer is not always right and we
let them know it from time to time."*

Alan Sugar

WARNING: BUYING A PRODUCT SOMETIMES gets you asked to do some very odd things. Although an instruction tells you to do something and a warning essentially tells you *not* to do something there is a kind of overlap. For example, a crazy piece of text in the manual for a Nikkai television set starts with the word *"warning"*, but is also in the nature of an instruction in the way that it is phrased: *"WARNING – do not watch television programmes or turn your TV set on for your own and others safety"*. Why it should make this either a warning or an instruction is another matter. Maybe if it listed specific programmes not to watch that would be different – "Dinner, dinner, dinner" and "Relocate me now" I can live without, though I may have those titles a little muddled.

Consider warnings: and let me start with an anecdote. When my son competed in a marathon in Iceland I travelled with him and we spent the day before the event on a coach trip. Amidst the awesome countryside we walked up a beautiful waterfall, it twisted and turned dropping steeply and dramatically. An American in the group expressed amazement that we were allowed to go along the narrow path with a long, sheer, unprotected drop to the falls below. "There is not even a warning sign" he said. The guide smiled as she replied, saying "In Iceland the whole country is dangerous – we know this and don't need to put up signs every few paces to remind us." In fact she found the very idea amusing and chuckled about it for some time. She had a point, too, but some things do need a warning though perhaps in this litigious age it is all rather overdone. For instance, practically everything you might put even near your mouth these days warns that it could contain "traces of nuts", not in many instances because there is a real chance it will, but "just in case".

Worcestershire road sign forewarns of:
Accident improvement roadworks

Heparin is drug used to thin the blood – an anticoagulant to be accurate. You inject it – with a syringe. That's the sort of thing that has the needle-phobic hitting a hundred decibels and leaving the doctor's surgery at speed. Many people are wary of a syringe, so why does the Fragmin syringe (the one with the catchy designation 2500IU/0.2ML) feel the need to tell people *"Do not swallow"*? Is there anyone needing heparin or any other drug who has ever in the history of the world looked at a syringe and said to themselves *Looks like a tasty snack, let's swallow it down?* I am sure I'm not the only one to think that the answer to that is no.

Sometimes instructions simply defy all logic. They are clearly wrong and yet it is impossible to think of any way that they could have been written; they contain no typos, appear not to have used a wrong word, they are just weird. Such is one of many instructions with the Raydon drill: *"The machine must be used with the attractive woman of security"*. What? The only explanation I can think of is that some feminine vision of loveliness walked by just as someone wrote this.

As part of the instructions for operating a keel lifting mechanism on a yacht, you are told to: *"Unscrew the bolt THM8 located at the end of the endless screw"*. It sounds like it may take some time to find the end and this seems to cast doubt on just how straightforward the rest of the instructions are likely to be. Indeed, that is a serious point. Instructions are important, getting them wrong can waste your time (assembling something takes hours), inconvenience you (something you have assembled falls apart) or seriously damage your health (if, say, you took the wrong medicine). If there is obvious evidence that the instructions were written with half an eye on a magazine during the writer's tea break and not checked at all, then we can have little confidence in them. I would go further: such errors can seriously dilute the image of an organisation – an image, no doubt, that they have worked hard to establish.

Label: **To remove scissors from pack, carefully cut cable tie using scissors**

Modern technology is truly wonderful, but there can be snags and it certainly presents many of us with a continuing learning curve. A friend in the computer industry asked to define the phrase "user friendly", told me "I suppose it means something is very, very complicated, but not as complicated as next year's model will be". Some gadgets certainly take a bit of getting used to, especially if there isn't a teenager in the house to explain. They can also take some time to set up and get going. Working through the instructions on an iPod (that's a music playing thingamajig if you are any sort of Luddite), one user found the screen displaying *"iPod disabled. Try again in 21,668,172 minutes"*. "Take some time to set up," did I say? That's more than 41 years! And I for one am too old to buy anything that needs that long to get it working.

But technology apart, nothing seems to be immune to confusion like this. Putty is pretty important – without it all your windows would fall out. It needs some care in use and evidently using it can involve considerable personal discomfort: one tin says *"Remove skin before use"*.

It is clearly important that children do not play with things that will do them harm and a classic warning is one about the danger of young children swallowing things. But isn't the following taking care in this area to absurdity: *"Not suitable for children under 3 years because of small parts"*. What product did this appear on? It was a foot wide, solid, one-piece, surely utterly unswallowable Frisbee. But perhaps you can't be too careful. Good old fashioned children's toys like Frisbees are declining in popularity in face of modern, and usually electronic, alternatives. Unless something buzzes, lights up or simulates killing voracious alien hordes, then it increasingly has no appeal. But there may be another reason. I think I've discovered the cause of the decline of one traditional toy: a skipping rope labelled *"Keep out of the reach of children"*.

Sign at Tring Angling Club:
No fishing

This next is not really a classic warning, but I like the thought of what one customer at a supermarket pharmacy counter buying a cream labelled "For external use only" reported, as the cash point flashed up the amount of money owing it also displayed the slogan *"Making life taste better"*.

Some dangers need explicit warnings. Railway companies thus display signs listing what to do in the event of an emergency. In the west of England, carriages display a notice about evacuating the train. It begins *"Strike the emergency door release panel with a fist (located above the exterior door)"*. In a real emergency I would have thought it mattered little what you whacked it with, but as it is evidently so important, it is good of them to provide a fist for you to do it with.

I have a friend whose garden has become a squat for foxes, indeed urban foxes are a widespread problem these days. One suggested antidote is a device that emits an ultra-sonic tone that only animals like foxes can hear and which it is claimed they dislike and move away from. So far, for such devices and various other cures my friend has only one comment – "Doesn't work". Well, maybe I have discovered why that is. On one such sound device is a helpful label *"This product will not work with deaf foxes*". No, really? But if the wretched creatures in my friend's garden are deaf, why do they bark at each other all night and keep the whole neighbourhood awake? If they are deaf maybe they could be taught sign language. My friend is still seeking a solution; suggestions on a postcard please.

A display of mirrors in one supermarket is labelled "*All-purpose mirrors*". That will be reflecting an image and, and... I am obviously very limited in my view of mirrors as it seems to me that they only have one use. Be that as it may there is surely no great inherent danger in a mirror, other than the guarantee of seven years of rubbish luck if you break one. Maybe there is more danger when they are electrical. The Elegance Touch-control illuminated beauty mirror includes amongst a wide range of instructions this one: "*Never use while sleeping*". What, not even if you are dreaming of combing your hair? Almost as mystifying is the instruction on a refrigerator explaining that "*The temperature control is located inside the fridge and as a safety feature can only be adjusted with door closed*". One wonders if this just sort of occurred to them or if there has been a rash of people getting stuck inside their new fridges. Very odd; indeed there seems to be no way round it. Other oddities refer to use. For example, one may wonder why a set of screwdrivers should be marked "*Not for pacemaker users or for use during pregnancy*". I have no clue as to what link might exist between screwdrivers and pacemakers, but perhaps the manufacturers feel that once you are pregnant then the screwing should stop for a while.

Label on a baby's teething ring:
Do not iron

The concept of food miles is a valid environmental issue. Transporting something half way across the world when there are fields of it growing down the road can involve costs in money and to the environment which are both substantial and unnecessary. Some customers want to avoid this and like to see the source of food labelled. But accurately please. In an ASDA supermarket a display of water melons was clearly marked "*Produce of more than one country*"; maybe they grow the fruit in one place and add the water in another.

Alchemy shampoo has various "*flavours*": one is noted as being for "*sensitive scalps only*", another "*for everyone*". No point in buying the special one then, I wonder if it costs more than the other. Anyway this seems to me to be one area of many where choice has gone mad; just how many kinds of shampoo need to exist? Other odd instructions and warnings include:

- A riding hat labelled *"Keep out of direct sunlight"*
- On a restaurant window: *"Prior notice is required for all reservations"*
- *"This label indicates that the package contains genuine Microsoft Product"* This then goes on to request that you email Microsoft *"if the label is missing"*
- *"Harmful if swallowed"* (on a brass three-pronged fishing lure)
- *"This product is not intended for use as a dental drill"* (on a large carpenter's drill)
- *"Do not use as a ladder"* (on a small CD rack)
- *"... cannot protect any part of the body they do not cover"* (on cyclists' shin guards).

Sign on gates near Exeter:
Warning – these gates may close without warning.
Actually, the notice suggests no, they won't.

A safety intercom on board the train from the airport into Brisbane suggests you *"Speak when light flashes"*; fair enough, but is it useful to repeat that, as it does, in braille? Maybe Australian railway sign writers are not too good at it; in Melbourne there are train carriages displaying a notice saying *"Power operated doors. When tone sounds open doors by hand"*. Also in Melbourne, a notice was seen instructing students at the university to *"Please put one-sided paper in box below for recycling"*. You surely don't need to have had a university education to know that paper is two-sided.

Growing things in your garden to augment your food supplies is clearly an activity undertaken by some pretty stupid people, at least if the label on some herb seeds is any guide. One said *"Warning: use stem and leaves only. Do not eat roots or potting mixture"*. I think if you want to eat potting mixture then you should select the box marked "Muesli". Cleaning instructions seem particularly prone to nonsense and ambiguity. For instance, a scarf labelled *"Dry clean only in cold water"* is hardly helping to clean it without damage, but at least it is not as bad as the instruction: *"Hand wash in warm water with mild detergent. Do not spin dry"* – which bizarrely appeared on a dog kennel.

Theft in stores is sadly rife these days. So, like many stores, Sainsbury's fit many of the more expensive products with security tags. Clever little gadgets they are too, and any inattentive shoplifter will find they set off an alarm if they try to take one out of the shop without paying. Usually they are taken off the goods at the checkout, but evidently not always: the Braun electric toothbrush is labelled *"Warning! This product is fitted with a security device which is NOT MICROWAVABLE"*. Possibly there are people who take such security devices home and must be warned not to microwave them; but why would they want to? Perhaps it's the toothbrushes some odd sub-group of shoppers wants to microwave, in which case they must be warned to take the security device off before doing so. But as the devices usually remain in the shop it all seems somewhat unnecessary. How on earth such an inappropriate warning gets onto a product must remain a mystery. One more thing about toothbrushes, a Sonic Plakway toothbrush is labelled "*Never use while sleeping*". Presumably it is even worse to brush your teeth in your sleep while looking at yourself in an Elegance Touch-control illuminated beauty mirror whilst doing so. Maybe you really should not use the mirror whilst asleep, so perhaps they are failing in their duty not to tell people not to use it while juggling flaming torches (distracted, you'll drop them and burn holes in the carpet), shopping or a thousand and one other things.

And before we leave the subject, here's one more thing about microwaves: if you have a certain model made by AEG, it tells you "*Do not use the microwave oven for drying pets*". This seems to me to be utterly unnecessary, but given some newspaper stories of animal cruelty, perhaps it's not. Mind you there are pets and pets. In South America people eat guinea pigs and maybe they cook them in a microwave for a quick meaty snack; but guinea pig is something I have never fancied since I was told that they are very tasty but rather spoiled by the fur sticking to the roof of your mouth.

Notice on Paddington station:
Passengers must stay with their luggage at all times or they will be taken away and destroyed.
Fear not: I don't think this means there's a gallows under Platform 8, it is just badly worded.

Some instructions must surely be noted very carefully as to say that the ramifications of not doing so are wide ranging is a huge understatement. A solar battery charger tells users it will *"keep the whole solar system in proper working condition"*. That's a relief – it seems that we are safe from spiralling into the Sun for a while longer. Television watching used to be just a matter of clicking a switch, now satellite and cable link us to a multitude of channels, pipe in movies and gives us the ability to record programmes and much more. The remote control is a link to another world; indeed one such suddenly prompted an on screen message saying *"You are receiving an update to your service. The Remote Control will not work for a few moments. To clear this message please press OK on the remote"*. That's the *"will not work"* remote, one presumes.

Following all these instructions is hard work and has given me a thirst. Getting a drink, I discover that Tzu Sparkling Apple tells you to *"Refrigerate after opening and consume immediately"* – deciding which to do first takes me long enough to make me even thirstier.

> Notice to those hiring a village hall:
> **Would all people using the village hall please put disposable nappies in the bin outside.**

Then there are instructions about using the instructions as it were. Do railway stations have a series of signs "in stock", as it were, that they can put up as appropriate? It seems likely, but if so what exactly is the one seen at Bedford station trying to achieve? It says: *"The information screens may be showing the wrong information at present"*, which, especially given that word *"may"*, is surely more likely to misinform and annoy passengers than a blank screen.

All websites need regular updating and maintenance and sometimes this demands that they are closed for a while. It is polite to advise customers of this, just as car manufacturer Hyundi do saying: *"This page is temporarily closed due to system maintenance. We hope to reopen this page at the soonest time. Thank you for kind understanding."* That may show signs of less than perfect translation but it is still clear, though it is rather spoilt by the unthinking addition of the stock slogan – *"Hyundi, always there for you"*. This is another example of writing on automatic pilot and not thinking about context, clarity... or anything else really. In this case there seems to be a standard slogan that is added to everything; even when it is clearly not the right place to do so.

> Instructions with a pair of baby socks:
> **wash and dry separately.**

Websites seem particularly prone to spouting nonsense, and so too does email promotion. Virgin Media amongst others have a line on one such saying "*Click here if you cannot see this email*". If I couldn't see it how could I... enough. I think it means that if you cannot see certain pictures and graphics then you should click. It which case why not be specific – what is it about communication on computers that means it is so often abbreviated to the point of being unintelligible? Actually be warned, some such messages are just a way of moving you from the one page email into a website which has even more blandishments to prompt you to look further and, of course, ultimately to buy.

Earlier I mentioned messages directed mainly for the safety of children, and something like the danger of a child suffocating on a plastic bag is worth every reminder going to get people not to leave one lying about. Mermaids hair products have printed a note about bags saying "*Dispose of safely. Please retain for reference*". Perhaps the word "dispose" should have been "file". Choking crops up regularly too, with warnings about that especially in evidence when something has small components (like a Frisbee). Paperchase even puts a warning on a purse with a label that says: "*WARNING. Choking hazard – not suitable for children under 36 years*". Perhaps some people never grow up.

Even something as apparently simple as a refrigerator comes with detailed instructions. This is not as bad as AEG, mentioned earlier, but a Miele model wants you to know exactly how to store things in it, saying "*... the coldest area is directly above the PerfectFresh zone*", going on at once to add, "*however the PerfectFresh zone is even colder*". Well of course it is, otherwise it would not warrant the name PerfectFresh.

> Beechams All-in-One cold cure tells users to
> **take two pills at a time**.

Possibly the ultimate ambiguity is the instruction given by the online magazine *Universe Today* as a caption below an image of the planet Jupiter. It said simply "*Click for full size image*"; I hope the day someone does that is not the day the world ends.

As well as immediate instructions such as push this, turn that or shake vigorously, some manufacturers take the trouble to give you background information. Mortain produce insecticide and their website tells you that "*Flies start to breed within 48 hours of completing their life cycle"*. Wait a moment, that seems to imply no more flies and no need for the insecticide designed to kill them. Or does necrophilia actually work for dead flies?

Food often seems to have slightly odd instructions, so much so that following them to the letter would cook up more than a few problems... and some odd meals. Much food is bought frozen these days, but take care especially with the fruit pudding labelled *"Defrost thoroughly before cooking in a refrigerator"*.

Despite reducing services on a regular basis and delivering a somewhat erratic service (this morning my post brought me an envelope that was posted first class less than ten miles away 14 days ago), the Royal Mail have thousands of post boxes around the country – many have two posting slots and amongst those some are labelled: *"Please Use Both Letterboxes"*. Even more bizarre, in Australia the main Post Office in Canberra has no less four posting slots. One is labelled *"Express"*, the other three all say *"All other mail"*, while the Post Office in Wokingham has three slots side by side each individually labelled *"This box has the latest collection in this area"*; though not if one of the others is emptied first presumably.

Roundup weed killer label:
Avoid contact with the environment

Let's applaud anyone who keeps things simple. A CircoStream oven advertisement in the *Good Housekeeping* magazine begins: *"Neff's CircoStream doesn't have complicated function – just simple one-touch controls, including 52 cooking programmes..."*. So for a start you need one-touch multiplied by 52 and already it sounds not so simple. No applause there then.

Some things we buy are out and out dangerous. Power tools come into this category, at least for a DIY incompetent like myself, and so too does a chain saw. One such offers the warning instruction: *"Always stand on one side while cutting, allowing plenty of space for a severed limb to fall without causing injury"*. Take heed: as if a severed limb isn't injury enough, you would not want to stand wrongly and risk still more injury. I saw this reported in a magazine by a lady who had given a chain saw to her husband for a birthday present; perhaps she thought his using it was less costly than a divorce.

Cooking is a real skill, though it is one I have largely failed to grasp and perhaps I am not alone as the sales of pre-cooked meals increases all the time. Like all the supermarkets, Somerfield sells cooked chicken, but with a difference: theirs comes with the instruction *"shake well before use"*. And a sign on a snack dispensing machine at Trinity College of Music says *"Please keep this area clear of food and people at all times"*; if this instruction is obeyed, presumably the snacks endlessly awaiting dispensing are growing whiskers or the machine is always empty.

There's more: the instructions for the Packard Bell PC tell you to keep it at least 30 centimetres away from a mobile phone. I am not sure why but I am pretty sure that it would be easier to move the phone.

Sign at farm gate:

Bag your own manure.

Are they collecting or selling?

Parking your car can be a problem. You often can't find a place and if you can it is expensive and if you don't buy a ticket it is even more expensive because you are clamped or towed away. The powers that be do not make the grizzly process any easier. A car park in Bristol allows you pay with a credit card, and that's convenient for some, but on the ticket machine it says: "*For credit card transactions please follow the instructions below*". Immediately underneath is another sign saying: "*Operating Instructions – See Above*". Every word is capitalised so it must be right. Don't stand there too long trying to work it out or you will go back to your car to find you've got a penalty ticket. This reminds my butterfly mind of a sign seen on a toll road in Oklahoma which said: "*Failure to Pay Toll Strictly*

Enforced". That's a form of wording that I'd like to see the equivalent of in car parks that I use.

Washing instruction are important, you do not want things to shrink or suffer in some other way, but what is one to make of a bed sheet from House of Fraser the packet of which advises purchasers to wash it inside out, or of a Timberland reversible jacket with the same instruction? In the case of the jacket some literally minded soul may be standing by their washing machine as I write this endlessly turning the jacket one way and the other and wondering what to do next. Impossible it may be to turn a sheet inside out, but some instructions simply defy any kind of explanation: a packet of condoms from Sainsbury states on the packet "*Please remove prior to putting in the microwave*". As opposed to climbing in while wearing one, perhaps? One wonders what the logic is for any mention of microwaves at all, unless the condoms are designed specially to use on a hot date.

Finally let me mention two more products whose instruction writers should go on the naughty step. The first is one we have all heard of which plays it really safe in face of likely idiot behaviour. The iPhone manual tells you "*Do not drop, disassemble, open, crush, bend, deform, puncture, shred, microwave, incinerate, paint or insert foreign objects into iPhone*". Someone was making good use of the Thesaurus, leaving no stone unturned, covering all the bases and... sorry RCD (that's rampant comprehensiveness disorder) is apparently infectious. Secondly, I came across a product I did not know – no, make that I did not dream existed: a glow in the dark toilet roll. There must be people who want such an item as there it is, on sale in full view. It does seem to me to have a significant drawback. The instructions say *"This is a novelty item. Glow in the dark coating can rub off the toilet roll. It is not dangerous, but please ensure you wash your hands thoroughly after use"*. Apart from disliking the very idea of a coating which rubs off in this fashion, it occurs to me that your hands are not the only spot on which the luminescence might end up. Indeed enthusiastic use could get it noticed later in situations where it might, just possibly, introduce an element of considerable embarrassment – *Are you radioactive, or just pleased to see me?*

As a final comment on instructions, maybe Sainsbury's have the right idea. A packet of their cod fillets simply advises *"Cook any way you choose"*. That at least I understand... even if I don't know how to decide what to do.

Seriously... be warned

Clearly there is a need for care as you read instructions. Some errors made are just silly and unlikely to lead you astray or put you in danger, though a few could do so and it is an area where product purveyors should pay greater attention.

Perhaps the greatest error here is when there are no instructions at all. All manner of goods seem to have instructions that are fine as far as they go, but have yawning gaps in them. You are doing just great assembling something, for instance, and then left with absolutely no idea how to get from step 10 to step 11. Maybe we should complain more and standards might rise. Certainly it is easier for a company to double check what their printed instructions say rather than have endless phone calls to deal with – all complaining and all wanting an answer to the same question. Serve them right perhaps, but better all round to get it right in the first place.

INTERLUDE

Some comments about products may be entirely clear yet are still inaccurate. For instance the word "best" is used a good deal where perhaps it actually means "one of the best". But one thing annoys me enormously, and it pains me to say so because it comes from the world of books which I love. Like many people who love books, I have certain authors whose books I always want to read; a new title from such a favourite is a treat and there are things I buy without question. I went out recently and bought such a book, pretty much on its listed publication date. An original paperback, this was its first appearance, yet across the top of its cover were the words *"His new number-one bestseller"*. But manifestly, at this stage it's not. It's not in the charts now and it certainly wasn't however long ago the jacket was designed and the book printed. You see this a good deal. It may come to be true but the publishers are, in my view, jumping the gun. Perhaps such a statement should carry a disclaimer: "His new bestseller. **Please note this is a prediction"*. Saying that may be more accurate, but I doubt it will happen; it does not have the same ring.

I am also tempted to have a go at bookshops, but I want them to stock this title by the crate so I will be gentle. Dear bookseller, when you have a display marked "New" I find them very useful and like to look to see what's newly published. I do find it very off-putting, though, if such a display is packed with titles that have been out for months. Have a look occasionally and update things. Maybe our definitions of "new" differ, but I think that would be better. Sometimes logic is breached for "good" reason or at least one I can understand, *Harry Potter and the Deathly Hallows* was published in 2008, but is up there as "new" with the final film on release. Just wait for the long awaited film of *The Hobbit*; the book was published in 1937, but I bet it's about to acquire a "new" label.

6. TIME, BUT NOT AS WE KNOW IT

A moment or two of confusion

"Eternity's a terrible thought,
I mean where's it going to end?"

Tom Stoppard

THE LATE DOUGLAS ADAMS, AUTHOR of *The Hitchhikers Guide to the Galaxy*, wrote that "time is an illusion", and evidently practised what he preached, always delivering work late to his publishers and being quoted as saying "I love deadlines, I love the whooshing noise they make as they go by". So if I am late delivering this book then I'm in good company. Albert Einstein made us realise that time is relative, but sometimes a degree of accuracy and conventional adherence to the everyday way we work in hours, days, months and the like would be a help to achieving understanding. Sadly all too often that adherence is not in evidence.

This is an area where there seem to be many misprints, yet some are so obviously wrong that it reinforces the point about communicating with customers needing a bit of care and checking. How can

Paypal, an organisation providing a sophisticated online payment system, tell a customer *"Your credit card that ends in 2235 will expire soon"* then go on to suggest that they go online and sort it out to *"avoid any interruption to your service"*. Well, if they are to be believed the card is good for well over two centuries yet, so they can make a cup of tea first as there's apparently no hurry. Or is the implication more ominous? Perhaps customers need to be given plenty of warning because logging in and contacting them is, as with all too many organisations, a tad slow. *Please remain connected. You are the 37,380,221st person in the queue and waiting time is now only 96 years.* You can tell I am making that up as in reality there would be a "your contact is important to us" message in there somewhere.

This sort of thing is no doubt all down to computers. But computers only do what you tell them – even the one that famously translated "Out of sight, out of mind" as "Invisible idiot" – so when some idiot put in the year 2235 then of course, unchecked, the computer knew no different and continued to churn out the error.

Airport sign:
Shuttles leave every half hour on the hour

The far future crops up a good deal in messages. A pack of Hovis bread yeast states *"Best before Mar 10 9075"*. Personally, I have no idea how long yeast lasts – maybe the date is correct, though the more pessimistic bread makers may doubt that the human race will still be around by then to eat bread or anything else. Actually it has already been around rather longer than you might think if you believe an advertisement for Penguin Hutchinson Reference Suite CD-ROM (long gone now, I suspect) but it claimed to cover *"human history from 500 million BC to the present day"*. We have been around long enough to invent best consumed by dates: a pack of Cripps Nubake traditional English muffins is evidently *"best before 30 February"*; so will presumably stay fresh until after some sort of major international calendar revision. As a mild adjustment to British Summer Time has been debated for many years, I would not hold your breath.

If you use an iPhone, though they change as you watch, some certainly allow you to enter dates of birth for contacts from the birth of Christ right on to thousands of years beyond the present. The iPhone is certainly a wonderful gadget, yet such things hardly have long lives and the chances of someone still using one by the time it is appropriate to enter a birth date in, say, the year 3087 must be remote. This sort of thing occurs elsewhere. Yahoo tells those who register for Yahoo mail *"You cannot use birthdate more than 150 years ago"*. Even for dates a bit short of that they seem to be targeting silver surfers.

Some things go even further back: BoardTracker.com allows an advanced search through the last 6142 years of internet posting, allowing you access to an early prehistoric version of the web, I guess. Perhaps all those cartoons of Stone Age man dragging women by the hair miss out the moment when they went on line to find a date. Always with the internet, security is a serious issue and like many internet companies nti has a user policy and things to say about "abuse of the services". Here they make it clear that *"You must not disclose your password or user ID to any one else. Your account can only be used for a single internet session at any one time and for not more than 24 hours in any one day"*. They obviously have some customers on a planet orbiting Alpha Centuri who ignore this as they wave their tentacles and use the service throughout a much longer day.

A sign reported in a Chinese takeaway asks you to note that: *"Every dish is instantly cooked to order, therefore short delays may occur"*, but any kind of delay, even a short one, makes it less than instant – so time is definitely relative, something that is always shown by time seeming to go more slowly when you are in a queue.

Sign on Richmond Park gates:
**These gates will close ½ an hour before
closing time.**

Another claim that involves 24 hours comes from Tesco Extra Care mouthwash, which is a boon if your breath smells because it provides *"24 hour action"*. So one quick rinse and you are right for the day. Wrong. It also says on the packet *"when used twice daily"*. Not so good then, and the inattentive could well feel short changed. It must be bad enough having smelly breath without also knowing that you cannot even buy an item of basic toiletry without being misled. This is surely a case of a catchy slogan (about 24 hours) overriding clarity and some would say honesty too.

I am writing this on a laptop computer and, so far, it has worked well. Such things are pretty reliable these days and I like to think this is because of the care and attention that is lavished on them before they hit the shops. My computer is not a Hewlett Packard (though my printer is an HP) which appear to be exceptional in regard to testing. One advertisement describes how they *"provide the latest and most reliable technology for small businesses today"*. It goes on to say that every one of their notebooks is *"subjected to 95,000 hours of rigorous testing"*. Forgive me, but computers become out dated quickly enough already, so I don't really want one that is 11 years old as it comes out of the box thank you very much, however reliable that may make it. For the record, I am working on a Dell machine and it has always performed well. I do rather wonder about the company, however, as their online ordering process, which tells you the company is subject to US export compliance procedures, then asks you various questions. Fair enough, you may say, but one is: *"Will the product(s) be used in conjunction with weapons of mass destruction i.e. nuclear applications, missile technology, or chemical or biological weapons purposes?"* which demands a Yes/No answer. In my case the answer is "no", but I can't help wondering what is going on here. Do they want to identify terrorists as a niche market, or if someone answers "yes" do they just want to have early warning to get themselves to the bomb shelter in the basement? Sorry, I digress – let's go back to time related examples.

On computer screen:
Time remaining for print job
about 2033406812 hours –
that's a whole forest gone
(though it is only an estimate).

Let's focus more on manageable spans of time for a moment. The UK Sleep Council has an insomnia helpline, so you might think that you need never lie awake alone again. Imagine someone can't sleep. They watch the late night movie, they make endless cups of tea (and even have the wits to make sure they use decaffeinated teabags), but sleep won't come and finally, in desperation, they phone the help line. A recorded message says *"The insomnia helpline aims to advise and reassure those who are having trouble sleeping. Don't be alone – phone the helpline... Monday to Friday, 6.00 p.m. to 8.00 p.m."* Is this a misprint or is the line really only available for a couple of hours each day when most people are actually *wanting* to be awake? It doesn't seem very reassuring and it is certainly no use at 3.00 a.m.

Notice on TV screen:

Yesterday will return tomorrow at 7 a.m.

(actually, rather disappointingly, "Yesterday" is part of the History channel).

Some things last longer than others, and claims are made about just a few products that defy imagination. The Meta Thatcham MC1 motorbike alarm sounds like a good product, and a good idea too, given the present day crime rate; now it is even better as the manufacturer has *"extended our free 'lifetime guarantee' on this product"*. For riders who fear a fatal accident, this must be a comforting thought. Not quite a lifetime, but clearly too long is this next one. Faced with contaminated supplies, a safety conscious Anglian Water asked customers to *"boil tap water for up to 10 days"*. If you once noticed a lot of cloud over East Anglia it was probably the steam.

If are fed up with road works slowing your car journeys, if you twitch every time you drive past rows of cones and see no signs of any reason for them to be there, then at least this notice, which appeared on a road in Wales, is honest. It simply said *"Slow construction ahead"*. Appropriate enough, as it sometimes seems as if time slows to a crawl in a contra flow and most road works seem to take twice the time to complete as is billed at the side of the road.

Waitrose Christmas turkey cooking instructions:
approximate cooking time... 2 hours and sixty minutes

We all know what a pain in the neck it can be to get some piece of household equipment repaired or serviced. Many suppliers will not give you a visit day with any accuracy, much less tell whether they will call in the morning or afternoon or fix a specific time.

Some do aim to do better: Miele promises *"Should you request a Miele engineer to visit, we are able to provide you with the time slot and name of engineer that will visit after 4.30 the day before"*. This is truly confusing. After all a week on Wednesday is after 4.30 yesterday, but perhaps they mean that if you are sitting there waiting patiently today no one will come and you should have been at home the day before. No wonder my dish washer doesn't work.

For those contemplating divorce perhaps,
a sign in a Jeweller's shop window offers for sale:
Eternity rings and half-eternity rings

Here's something festive for you. Or is it? Special Christmas packs of Lyons mince pies carry the tag line *"Great for Christmas"*; certainly this is a traditional Christmas item – so why does the small print say *"Best before 17 November"*? This was probably organised by whoever it is who arranges for me to receive my first catalogue of Christmas cards through the post in July. In similar vein a child's sweater featuring the slogan *"My first Christmas"* is labelled as suitable for children *"from 18 – 24 months old"*.

If you are ever caught short, don't head for the public toilet in Kips Bay Library, New York where a sign says *"Restroom closes 15 minutes before closing"*.

Best just assume it is never open and go elsewhere. This error occurs despite the fact that the library doubtless contains a book or two on writing English and the hushed environment surely being conducive to taking a moment to check things. But American English is a little weird: they don't use the word fortnight, write dates the wrong way round and pronounce words like aluminium and tomato in an odd way, so perhaps such things are only to be expected.

Online message:

Thank you for contacting Ikea. We will respond within the next 24 hours, if not sooner

---

Sometimes you get the impression that those drawing our attention to time issues actually don't expect us to understand them. If you buy a gadget from pixmania.com you can choose to have it delivered by Standard or Express delivery. This they explain thus: Standard delivery costs £6.00 and takes 2 – 3 days; alternatively, Express delivery costs £10.10 and takes... 48 – 72 hours. Did I write "alternatively"? I wonder how many inattentive customers in a hurry click "Express" and end up paying more for nothing. A misprint or a con, I wonder, and does it represent a choice?

Some instructions are time based: for instance if you are replacing a broken window pane and need some putty, one brand tells you that *"Painting must be carried out within 28 days of application"* but it also says *"Allow 28 days for surface of putty to sufficiently harden before overpainting"*. Both instructions can't be right. Surely you need some sort of gap when it is actually right – and possible to do the painting; or is this a reluctant DIYers charter to leave the job half done? Oh, and by the way, what is this "overpainting" business? Perhaps there is somewhere in the multiverse where paint is put on *under* the surface of things. The railways use this kind of word too: asking passengers to cross platforms *"by the overbridge"* presumably to avoid confusion with all those bridges that go underneath the platforms.

Packaging for Vicks Sinex spray:

Do not sue Vicks Sinex for longer than 7 days without medical advice"

– what, not even if it seriously misinforms you?

We all need to be on our guard for computer viruses and the like and having software to protect you makes good sense. You need to keep your software up to date too, as new viruses are being created as you watch. Norton advised one user: *"To continue using Norton Internet Security, please activate within 4915287 days"*. Surely updates need incorporating rapidly, suggesting that you wait upwards of 13,000 years hardly seems prudent. Will there be computers then or will people all *be* computers? It is an odd thought to see one provider of such software saying on their website: *"Users who have no internet or email access at all and cannot uninstall or shutdown ZoneAlarm, please click here"*. If you do manage to click you are given a phone number, one presumably unlikely to be overburdened with calls. Wait a minute, perhaps it means that there are some helplines you actually *can* contact easily.

If you feel like a break and go to the Hotel Lenno on Lake Como in Italy, you will find the many facilities include a *"Complimentary minibus to nearby Spa (approx. 3 metres)"*. Sounds like you will be there in no time at all. If you go to this hotel by car, be sure you have a current licence. The driving test is in two parts these days, and you need to take the theory one first: the UK Driving Standards Agency says *"You can normally book a theory test 24 hours a day, every day"*. But it adds *"Outside these hours you can make a 'pending' booking"*, which I guess means there is no such thing as a pending booking. Either that or there are learner drivers on Alpha Centuri.

Colgate toothpaste pack:
Clinically proven everyday protection against time.

Maybe the Colgate pack notice shown above indicates a route to eternal youth; probably not. Anyway, it reminds me of the regular offers I get through the mail from *Time Magazine* in envelopes marked *"Time – do not bend"*. Longevity is a welcome characteristic of many products. You don't want your shoes to wear out before you get down the garden path to the road or a CD to fail before it reaches the end of its first play, but what does this sign, seen in a shop window, mean: *"Lifetime guarantee for all watch batteries"*? A sign on the M25 around London tells drivers of a junction eight miles ahead, saying: *"Travel time 8 minutes"*. Alongside is another sign restricting speeds to 40 mph. Maybe they work together.

I cannot pretend to have any sympathy for creationists who think the world was formed just a blink of an eye ago in geological time, but I discover some products do accommodate their odd sense of the flow of time. The publisher Live and Learn Press produces a dinosaur pack for children saying *"Dinosaurs – every child seems to go through a stage of loving them!"* and suggesting firmly that *"Your child will learn all about these creatures"*. But they add, *"There is no reference to dates so you are free to insert your family's view of the age of the earth and when dinosaurs roamed it"*. How sweet, maybe there is another version in which dinosaurs discover fairies at the bottom of the garden. I confidently expect their next publication to be titled "A Guide to Twenty First Century Fossils". That said, maybe more suppliers should just leave their customer to work out the time implications themselves rather than confuse them with things like the notice in the Mary Rose Museum in Portsmouth which says *"This film lasts for four minutes and is repeated every 15 seconds"*. That is a statement that brings a whole new meaning to the words "fast forward".

The mention of ancient times and the age of dinosaurs reminds me of two more "time" examples of disinformation. First, why does merchandise sold to visitors to America's Grand Canyon boast that it was *"Established in 1919"*; I think even creationists might allow that it is a good bit older than that. Secondly, all this makes me wonder why Himalayan salt, billed as being some 250 million years old, has a sell by date on the pack? Surely a few more months can't hurt.

Let's end our focus on time with another notice that first proposes an impossible action and secondly shows what many of us feel, that time goes too fast (especially, in my experience, as we get older) – life rushing past is actually all down to the railways. See below.

Notice at Oxford railway station:
To speed up time, please use all available train doors to enter the train

---

Seriously ... be warned

Time is potentially something that customers will feel needs to be accurate. Punctuality is not so universally thought necessary these days and attitudes vary to it around the world. In Thailand, a country whose relaxed attitude I love, for example it is said that if you ask what Thai word is equivalent to manyana, a local will tell you there is no word with the same degree of urgency. Similarly, when I reprimanded a Thai friend for being late in meeting me, the answer was a slightly aggrieved, "But I am on time... my time". But for product claims we want a degree of accuracy.

In the next chapter we look at a variety of confusions around measurements. We can draw the main conclusion here immediately: faced with figures, in this case relating to time, suppliers should make sure that what is said is clear, unambiguous and actually helps people. Poor communications in this area should not just send guilty companies to the naughty step, it should, at worst, send customers in search of an alternative supplier.

INTERLUDE

What do others think?

Given the difficulty of being sure that what you buy is going to be good, a useful manifestation of our modern world is those web sites that accept people's views about products and allow others to read them before they buy, or don't buy, a similar thing.

Tripadvisor-type websites certainly claim to be a way of checking out whether something is good or rather just how good or bad it is. Some of what is said on them – good or bad – is doubtless an honest reflection of the feelings and experience of a previous customer. But probably we should mark them down a bit. Granted some people go over the top: their beer is served a touch less than icy and suddenly they are slagging off an entire hotel – *Makes downtown Lagos seem like paradise*. But more relevant here are the reports that exaggerate how good something is. Hotels are not the only "product" involved here, but let's take that as an example. As well as genuine reports, some will no doubt be placed by the hotel manager and their staff, friends and family; others will be put on by guests in return for some perk (a free dinner or round of drinks perhaps); some will be written by bored insomniacs who just fancy being nice as a break from more extensive surfing.

Not only can anyone join in, but there can be financial reasons for doing so. You can literally sit on the other side of the world from a hotel you have never stayed at, log in a positive report and get paid for doing so. Numbers of sites have requests to do this secreted within their content; one sometimes mentioned is Mechanical Turk, a site for seeking work. Have a look. So again you should be wary and if you find a guest report uses exactly the same words as the hotel's own website home page then you may be forgiven for thinking that maybe some cut and pasting has been going on.

7. WHAT'S THAT IN ELEPHANTS?

A failure to get the measure of things

"He uses statistics like a drunken man uses lamp posts, for support rather than illumination."

Andrew Lang

MINE'S A PINT. AND IF I say that in a pub, I expect a pint delivered with some degree of accuracy. Actually, I'm sure we all expect it to be spot on and this is an area where the standard glasses or tankards used allow that to happen pretty much every time. Measurements matter. You want a pint to be a pint, you want your medicine dosage to cure you and not kill you and the Beagle 2 mission controller wanted his capsule to land on Mars (and test whether there had ever been anything alive there), but some metric and imperial measurements had been muddled up and instead it crashed and relayed only an endless silence. Some £65 million wasted on an avoidable measurement screw-up. I bet any life they might have found there is still laughing.

Many people find numbers a touch confusing and, frankly, common practice makes it unsurprising. Depending on your age, you may consider your weight in pounds or stones, but never in kilograms despite the pressure to go metric. We resist this pressure in many ways, for instance buying jam in one pound jars and calling them 454 grams. Do some DIY and you will measure the girth of your plank in inches – *some two by four please* – but its length in metres. It's all a bit of a muddle. Thus everyday comparisons are sometimes used. *Which?* magazine favours whales, telling its readers that 50 million packets of bacon are eaten in the U.K. every year and that's "*the equivalent of 50 blue whales*". Surely pigs would have been a more appropriate benchmark. You would never get a whale in a sandwich, but maybe 50 whales is a tiny bit easier to imagine than 50 million packets. Maybe.

Elephants are more often favoured, with *The Guardian* telling us that the ice dropping off Greenland every year is equivalent to "*a billion elephants*". Not true, incidentally; if true then elephants weigh upwards of 300 tons apiece. And if elephants don't quite fit then other bizarre comparisons seem to come to mind: the British Potato Council tells us that we eat 38,000 tons of chips (in the U.K.) every week and then pick something truly indigestible saying that's the "*equivalent of almost 5500 double-decker buses*". I just love the fact of that word "almost" being in there;

perish the thought that we might think it was 5500 *complete* buses. I also love another comparison I saw somewhere, describing the amount of money Bill Gates is worth by saying that if he put it all under his mattress and fell out of bed it would take him 10 minutes to hit the floor!

Even if such descriptions are straightforward, a glitch in expressing it can confuse and misinform. Acer advertise a desktop computer saying "... *it occupies less than ten times the space of modern tower PCs*"; that could still make it about the size of a couple of filing cabinets, yet somehow I suspect they were trying to point out how compact it was. A similar feel is given by Nintendo: their web site states that: "... (the Wii) *launched in November and sold over two million units in as many months*". A period seems to be involved here of many thousands of years. Back to size: one version of Zip Firelighters is promoted as being a *"New improved cube shape"*. But can you change a cube without changing the rules of geometry?

So, numbers may present difficulties, nevertheless when we are communicated with as customers we can surely expect that because measurements matter to us, whether they relate to the fat content of a food or the physical size of something, they will be rendered in an understandable and accurate way. Not always true. The Alba PCD 730 CD player evidently weighs 320486 lbs. That's more than 16 tons and will have even a qualified removal firm ordering a crane. Don't order one of these on the basis that you collect it yourself, no matter how much cheaper that is. That may be wrong, simply an error, but at least it's so wrong it's pretty damn clear that it *is* wrong. Perhaps we can all guess at the range of sizes in which a typical kitchen bin liner comes, but most likely we want one to fit *our* particular bin, so what do we make of one labelled as *"120 x 190 x T-shirt"*; if you can translate that into inches then you have the oddest sense of both language and measurements. It's nonsense and probably a cut and paste error. And it's not helpful and, frankly, I for one am not buying any... and, before you ask, one cannot just have a look at the bag because the description was in a catalogue. The simplest measurement can be expressed in the oddest way. The Canon BJC printer is described as being *"about a 12-inch ruler long by half a 12-inch ruler wide"*; most of us can imagine 12 inches by six without involving rulers and then halving them.

Even the number one can be misused. Betty Crocker's products are billed as easy to prepare, presumably leading to names like "Betty Crocker's One-Step Pancakes", but on the back of the pack for that the cooking instructions suggest you follow *"these basic steps"*. There are four or five of them – naughty, naughty. Stephen Hawking is not the only person to work in imaginary numbers. A search on Raleigh's website advertising their range of bikes brought up the message: *"The search returned 3 results of which the top 10 are listed below"*. Imagine.

Advertisement for Thompson & Morgan
tomatoes says they are
Bred using traditional methods not genetics.
My knowledge of biology must be wrong then.

"Cooper Tyres – guaranteed to last up to 80,000 kilometres." Sounds good? Perhaps for a split second – until you realise that it can clearly mean that any number up to the 80,000 means the guarantee has been fulfilled however shiny your tyres get: *Sorry, guv, I know you've only been to the end of the road and back, but it does say "up to 80,000 kilometres" so we can't change them.* This kind of language may sometimes be a mistake, but one fancies that it is used all too cynically by those aiming to confuse and make something sound better than it is. It is a ploy also regularly used in regard to discounts. The store Halfords offered a sale on Sat Navs: *"Up to half price"*. Two pence off? If I had a quid for every time I have seen something like that, I could pay full price. The "up to" ploy is a bad one and all too often used. It has a close relative that is the "less than" ploy, a way of words that grammatically surely demands that there is a "less than *something*" in there somewhere. Often there is not and the *exotic taste*

sensation that is Cadbury's Turkish Delight (their words) goes a step beyond, saying that it is *"60% less fat, and always has been"*. Nonsensical? Confusing? Or designed to confuse? You decide.

Most often the "less than" tag is taken to refer to an earlier version of the same product, but it is often not clear; maybe some foods are compared with something else, but they would not actually say "Less fat than a chip pan" would they? Though having researched this book I do wonder. Actually, to be fair to Cadburys an asterisk led to some small print that made it clear that the "less than" referred, on a per gram basis, to *"the average of leading chocolate bars"*. No doubt this includes a good few bars with no Turkish Delight in them at all and I bet that it also includes a few that have less fat than… but we are getting into an infinite regression and I still feel it's misleading. If all this does not matter then presumably we can compare anything with anything else: maybe chocolate has less fat than chicken pate; or not.

Another ploy that merits the "less than" award for being less than honest with consumers is the increasing practice of manufacturers surreptitiously reducing the size of things. They can then make comforting statements about prices being held (usually in the face of enormous economic pressure), or even reduced, when in fact value for money and cost per pound or whatever has been slashed within an inch of its life. This surely qualifies as being sneaky if not downright dishonest and misleading. In evidence of this I saw a letter to a newspaper bemoaning this practice and offering proof in the form of the fact that you can now, allegedly, put a whole Cadbury's chocolate egg in your mouth in one go. Nibblers may not notice the reduction in size of this sort of item, but apparently those with a terminator style of eating certainly do.

Some manage to combine less and more together to produce something still more confusing. TomTom sat nav instructions rightly remind users that road layouts do not stay the same for ever, but they say *"Don't forget, roads change no less than and up to 15 per cent a year"*. It is good to know the level of change to expect and where would we be here without the precision added by using percentages? They will soon be telling us it's a new roundabout, a roundabout and a half, and half a roundabout and relating it all to how many beans make five. Another measure that evidently causes difficulty is degrees. This crops up in, amongst other contexts, luggage – the American Flyer Suiter 26-inch Wardrobe Valet (just how many words does it take to name a suitcase?) which has *"quiet, 360-degree spinning wheels"*. No surprise there then; I wonder if they use any wheels that spin less than 360 degrees – or more.

Weights can be important for all sorts of reasons. You can order this book from Amazon and it will be sent post free; but I doubt they would do that if it was inscribed on lead sheets, the mail cost would be too high. Of course Amazon sells all sorts of goods these days, certainly far more than books and CDs. Some items are of a nature which means the weight is quoted on the product description, and sometimes this is interesting. For instance, a vehicle reversing aid, whatever that is – in my case it's sometimes a wife shouting "Stop. STOP!!" – is available and noted as weighing two kilograms. Fair enough, but evidently when it is packed and shipped it weighs only 599 grams. Somehow that is inexplicably a lot less than the product *without* its packaging. Maybe this is linked in some mysterious way to their ability to offer free delivery.

So sometimes numbers and measurements can be wrong, badly phrased or confusing and, let's be honest, it must sometimes be difficult for whoever writes this stuff to get to grips with it and make sure it's correct. Poor dears. Maybe Holland & Barrett have the answer: just ignore the numbers and write the same thing after them all. Their flaxseed oil supplement comes in two strengths – 1000 or 500 milligrams – both tell you to "*Take one capsule twice a day*" adding that "*you should not exceed the stated dose*". Flaxseed has been cultivated for thousands of years and even a cursory trawl of the internet shows that it helps lower cholesterol, prevent heart disease, angina, and high blood pressure as well as reducing inflammation, correcting hormone related disorders and reversing infertility. Actually I think the word "may" preceded "help". Even so it sounds like a must-have addition to any medicine cabinet and presumably in the larger dose a couple of capsules a day is twice as likely to be a help as is its little brother. Perhaps if it is infertility you seek to correct, you get twins. The lack of precision simply astounds, and maybe there is still a danger that desperate would-be parents will exceed the stated dose.

Seriously, you cannot be too careful with medicines (or supplements either, for that matter) as almost anything has at least the possibility of side effects. These are what is known in medical circles as ADRs or Adverse Drug Reactions (and maybe the excuse "No, dear, I've got a headache" would be even more persuasive as "No, dear, I've got an adverse drug reaction"). Responsible pharmaceutical companies warn you of these and even, in many cases, tell you what to do if they occur: for example, if you take methotrexate (for your rheumatoid arthritis) it could evidently result, amongst other things, in a loss of consciousness, but, no worries, the literature with it counsels you to "... *tell your doctor immediately if you notice any side effects*". Or at least when you come round. Doesn't anyone read this sort of thing *before* it's printed and distributed?

Just as I was writing the paragraph above, I spotted a letter written to the *Daily Telegraph* in which someone told of spotting this line on what he described as his heart medicine: *"If your heartbeat becomes very slow or stops, go to hospital immediately"*. Hospital, he added, was more than 30 minutes away. The two things together justify some ranting: the pharmaceutical industry is one of most heavily regulated around and is also one of the most profitable. Surely they can afford someone to write and check such vital information who can avoid this sort of thing. After all, it is pretty difficult to tell your doctor that you have lost consciousness, but it is damned impossible to get yourself to hospital if your heart has stopped. I repeat – doesn't anyone read this sort of thing *before* it's printed and distributed? On the naughty step whoever wrote these examples.

More positively errors can sometimes make you feel better about yourself. An advertisement for a paintballing centre has a threatening armed figure proclaiming that *"0.95% of people fail"*. Do people really find it that easy? More often errors just leave you confused: Schloer fruit drink's label tells you it is *"Best served 100% chilled"*. What does that mean... as ice cubes? Numbers can give problems even when no specific number is involved: the hi-fi outfit Richer Sounds once advertised that *"some of our deals are finite in supply"*. I guess that will stop you being disappointed if something you want is no longer available at a bargain price, but it says "some" – what I wonder do they have an *infinite* quantity of, for goodness sake?

Precision is out there too. AT & T advise their customers of their internet download usage so that they can avoid going over their limit. One customer with a limit of 5120 megabytes was told he had so far used 24. – and then, after the decimal point, the figure was followed by no less than 45 further numbers! Did he really need to know to that level of precision? Almost certainly not. Let's not worry, though, as this gigantic number was followed by the explanatory phrase *"This usage summary is only an estimate"*. Some estimate. In a similar vein, Seafair Milford Haven measure the boats they book into moorings, or at least they did for one yacht owner who it told that his boat was 5.7911999999999999 metres long (and the beam was measured with a similar accuracy). Quite how they did that is a mystery, as even an atom of water on the side of the boat would change that degree of measurement.

Let's go back to weight for a moment. This causes problems all over the world. The New Zealand post office sells special boxes to make sending gifts easier. The different sizes each come with a maximum weight limit: a small one (140 x 130 x 25mm) specifies packing no more than 20 kilograms in it, yet if you filled it with a solid lump of the heaviest element known to man (something like iridium) it would weigh less than 10 kilograms. Perhaps they are just playing safe.

Recruitment advertisement:
7 ton delivery drivers wanted

All this number crunching is making me hot and sweaty. Correcting that I noticed that Sure Extreme Protection deodorant is *"Proven to work at 58C, the hottest temperature recorded on Earth"*. I presume they tested it at that temperature in the lab and did not stand by waiting until someone recorded the world's hottest ever temperature and then rushed off to test it wherever that was in the world. That apart, something is wrong with the numbers as the package also says *"Protect from sunlight and do not expose to temperatures exceeding 50C"*. Seems as if it might explode before you can prove it works at a higher temperature still. Thinking of ingredients, Munchy Seeds Pumpkin Mix packages state helpfully: *"Due to the nature of this product it may contain traces of natural materials"*, which simply begs the question, if there are traces in there of something natural – what does the rest of it consist of? Yuk.

There are certainly some numbers provided that seem accurate, but still give pause for thought. A pack of 10 Minute Maid cartons of fruit juice proclaims *"2 more boxes than other leading juice box 8-packs"*. Wow!

And, back to elephants, on a bag of Cadbury's Mini Eggs it states that *"1.25 billion Mini Eggs are produced every year. This is equivalent in weight to 625 African elephants"*. I can't help feeling that this fact is stated with some pride, but does it make you want to buy Mini Eggs? I'm not sure, though I firmly believe that a balanced diet is chocolate in both hands and that the word that links best to chocolate is compulsory.

On Hook Norton Haymaker Pale Ale label:
**Where progress is measured in
pints – Volume 500ml**

Finally, the "top elephant" prize for comparisons should go to Martin Symington, writing in *The Times* about the new Airbus: *"Fully laden the A380 holds 310,000 litres of fuel, enough to fill 21 road tankers... The aircraft's interior volume is 1570 cubic metres, the equivalent of 44 million ping-pong balls... removing all the seats from both decks would provide enough space for 10 squash courts... a freighter version, the A380F, will carry 150 tons of cargo – about the same as a herd of fully grown Asian elephants..."*. It went on in this vein until it was not in question that this plane is seriously *big*. Maybe I should work out how many paper clips weigh the same as this book to make it seem like a weighty tome.

Seriously ... be warned

It will all make sense in the end, no doubt – or not. But numbers do take a bit of working out. If there is a moral here it is not to believe everything you read and, faced with the sort of nonsense numbers quoted here, to do the maths; otherwise there is every likelihood that you will be misinformed, confused or frankly conned. Beware – especially if decimals or percentages are involved – and keep a calculator handy. A few moments spent working out that something is not what it seems could save you time, money or a long time with the wrong product and an angry bank manager.

One more thing about working things out: if you have a mind, look at www.simonkelk.co.uk/sizeofwales.html; here you can put in sizes of all sorts of things and what that is in elephants, London buses and a whole lot more is just a click away. Whatever company put the relevant software in my computer is helping all this too: I had a message when downloading something the other day that said that the task would *only* take 20,124,778 hours to complete Patience, patience. Besides, given a couple of thousand years, even I might learn to be numerate. Meantime there are plenty of companies out there that are innumerate, incompetent or, at worst and I suspect too often, actively using numbers to confuse you.

134

Now if you are by any chance in the Homebase store in East Grinstead you should: **"... use the red button to open the automatic doors",** or you could just turn over the page and move on to the next chapter.

INTERLUDE

Good intentions

There are certainly bad boys in the commercial world: some companies, like Enron, sink and destroy the lives of many as they do so; some take unwarranted risks and suffer for it, as Nick Leeson did; and others go into the language as Robert Maxwell did after stealing £400 million from his company's pension scheme and subjecting so many to a difficult retirement.

But many people and entities in business do try to do the right thing. In recent years many companies have taken to publishing a "mission statement", a succinct description of what they stand for and how they intend to operate. Many such statements seem simplistic, but if it focuses them in a purposeful way then having one may well be a good thing. For instance, here is what just a few companies say about themselves:

- *The Coca Cola Company exists to benefit and refresh everyone it touches.*
- Heinz says: *Our vision, quite simply, is to be the world's premier food company, offering nutritious, superior tasting foods to people everywhere.*

- Virgin: *We believe in making a difference. In our customers' eyes Virgin stands for value for money, quality, innovation, fun and a sense of competitive challenge.*

Perhaps such things seem a little trite, but most indicate that they have customers' satisfaction in mind. That attitude should apply to all customers, even those who are not their greatest fans; it was Bill Gates who said *"Your most unhappy customers are your greatest source of learning".*

So many want to get it right; maybe on the evidence here they should just make clear communication a higher priority. I think customers would like that.

8. MISCELLANEOUS MESS UPS

The bad, the worse and the downright unforgivable

"Every crowd has a silver lining."

P T Barnum

THE FAMOUS AMERICAN CIRCUS PROPRIETOR quoted above also reputedly coined the phrase that there is "one born every minute", meaning someone he could persuade to part with their money. Whether you are being tempted to purchase or just given advice, what is said to you can be as meaningless as the Californian road sign warning of *"Zero visibility possibility"*, as odd as the sign in an Edinburgh shop window advertising *"Free range furniture"*, or as unnecessary as the shampoo bottle labelled *"Caution – this not food"*. Actually, thinking about it I am worried about the second one of those: I just hate to think of battery farmed coffee tables – so cruel.

So there is more to consider.

A notice on an office door says *"Use this door only when entering/exiting"*. Doors do not have so many uses, so I'm not sure what that is all about. Presumably there is something they want to stop people using them for. Worse, the St James's Centre car park in Edinburgh has a sign that says *"Two cars must leave before one can enter"*; if this was there when the place was built then there have presumably never been any cars in it at all. Some warnings are just so silly. Care must be taken over anything given to children, of course, but why is a teddy bear labelled: *"Please remove all clothing before giving this item to a child"*. The mind boggles. Perhaps it should be advertised as "Teddy Bear – free sex instruction included". Others have an element of confusion to them, such as the label seen in Rymans on a pack of pens *"Permanent markers, with eraser"*, the wording of which is neatly contradictory.

Computers must be treated with a certain degree of care, but one at least comes with the warning *"Never hammer a nail into the battery pack"*. This seems to suggest that computer abuse happens in a pretty aggressive manner; and to think I worry if I give mine a tiny knock getting into the train. Hewlett Packard computer printer cartridges are big, solid plastic things but they still say *"Harmful if swallowed"*; better safe than sorry though, perhaps a few purchasers keep pets: a hippopotamus could certainly gulp it down. Something you *should* actually swallow also has an odd warning. On a packet of Paracetamol tablets is a warning saying that it *"Contains paracetamol"*. Well I should hope so. Another pill packet tells you to "*Swallow whole with a full glass of water*". Not possible. Let's guess – they mean a glassful of water, so don't be literal and risk curing your headache and cutting your throat to ribbons. Another pain killer from Medised for children cautions that the user should not operate heavy machinery or consume alcohol, while failing to mention why a two year old should be driving, say, a fork lift truck or fuelled by extra strong lager (that's the two year old fuelled, not the truck).

On a jar of Le Parfait pickled onions it says "*Do not consume products from an unsealed container*". While it is difficult to imagine people *ever* consuming onions or anything else from a sealed container it must mean a jar lasts for ever.

From New Zealand:
**It is dangerous to cross this bridge
when this notice is underwater**

"*Wash dark colours separately*" say the instructions for cleaning a shirt; but what do you do when the material in question has black and white stripes? "*Warning, danger of suffocation*" is a notice one sees on plastic bags and that, as I've said before, is sensible enough but why on earth do the same words appear on the safe in a hotel in Swindon? It's fixed in place and far, far too small to climb into. Perhaps it's... no, this is one where surely no explanation will make it any clearer.

In our high-tech world, cameras get cleverer and cleverer. The Sony Ericsson K800i can, like many these days, be set to take many pictures in rapid succession from one click, a feature that makes it ideal for taking pictures of, say, a speeding athlete. Uniquely perhaps this particular camera does this "... *from just before to just after you press the button*" Perhaps such an early start means you will never miss a crucial moment again. Aqueous Cream is a product designed to deal with hard skin on the feet. The manufacturers have great faith in it, so much so that they recommend that you "*Always take the container of Aqueous Cream with you even if it is empty*". This seems truly weird: but, hey, maybe it's something you only ever need to buy once. In a similar vein a can of shaving foam once said "*No animal testing or ingredients*", thus suggesting that more than one product works perfectly well though there is nothing in it.

A sign in a hospital in Cardiff, states "*Refuse to be put into the incinerator*". Dead right – resist all attempts to put you in, even though if you do get burnt you are in the right place for treatment. Maybe if they do treat burns victims there, they use Cetrimide cream. Though this is recommended only for "*minor burns*", on it a label advises users to "*Avoid contact with eyes, middle ear, brain and surrounding membranes*". How many people try to rub any sort of cream into their brains? I mean how could you? No explanation comes to mind, unless the person who wrote this already has brain damage caused by unthinking tinkering with their own.

Sign on the door of a New Mexico restaurant:
Come in. We're closed.

It is great to learn a foreign language and many companies sell aids to assist this, for instance courses on CDs and such like. One such company is the AA, who, when they are not busy keeping you waiting by the roadside in the pouring rain, sell a whole range of other useful stuff, much of it nothing to do with cars. The pack for one of their language courses says: "*With AA Essential Italian Deluxe you'll be reading, writing and speaking French in no time at all*". If this is true it conjures up the prospect of someone working long hours to acquire some fluency in Italian, booking a holiday and only on arriving in Rome discovering that no one understands what they say because they are speaking French. Actually that's not all, they don't specify hours of hard work at all but rather suggest proficiency comes in "*no time at all*". As one who can forget how to pronounce a foreign word I have repeatedly practised after, say, a five minute pause, I somehow doubt that. Before we leave this one, I do like the use of the word "essential" in the product name: it reminds me of the Sony Vaio laptop computer I had that told me to consider purchasing *"Optional Vaio essentials"*. That glowing description produced no additional business for Sony as I decided to go with the word "optional" rather than the "essential".

Even those selling things second hand have difficulty with description. A new student at the University of Warwick saw a sign on a notice board offering *"Essential course texts for sale. Never used"*. Perhaps it meant they were in good condition, perhaps they were not so essential or perhaps they were indeed essential and their original owner failed their exams dismally having not read them. We'll probably never know.

Nasty marks and stains can be a problem. Luckily, a wealth of cleaning products offer help. Stain Block says clearly on its aerosol can that it is *"Ideal for grease marks"*, but the details about using it then add that before you use it you should *"Ensure all surfaces are clean, dry and free from grease"*. Back to the shop with that one, I think, and onto the naughty step for whoever is responsible for it; perhaps Research and Development should have taken a little longer over its creation. But not as long as this: Seabrooke Potato Crisps is not, I think, a major brand and I think I know why that is. The packet informs the purchaser that the crisps have been *"Cooked in pure sunflower oil for 25 years"*. So perhaps however much you like them, by the time the shop gets any more in stock you will have forgotten all about them.

This winter I may be needing de-icer for my car if the weather is cold. Magic Ice Stops deals with ice and frost on your car windscreen but it seems it only works *"up to minus 15 degrees C"*. In England at least we can go through a whole year and not have a single day when the temperature falls that low; maybe it is designed for export – to Siberia.

Sign in hospital lift: **The fourth floor has been moved to the ninth floor.**

Radio Times exhorts you to watch a programme on ITV2 and presumably quotes information given to them by the channel in question. One programme is listed as a repeat, and that is common enough, but it also says *"It includes previously unseen footage"*. It can't be a riveting programme as this must mean no one watched it last time round; or maybe viewers only tuned in to watch the commercial breaks.

There seems to be no end to this sort of muddle. Why oh why do shoes bought from the Land's End catalogue have a warning label saying *"Do not eat"*? I'll just have to go back to betting people with the forfeit of eating my hat. Are you fit or like me could you do with taking more exercise? One way of achieving fitness, and avoid the gym, is to have your own exercise machine. A good one to choose is the Kettler Crosstrainer which, so its makers say, "... *makes exercise effortless*". On the one hand that is just what I want, but I suspect that, if it's true, it would not be doing me any good. The comedienne Joan Rivers has the right philosophy I think; she is reputed to have said: *"I don't exercise. If God had wanted me to bend down he'd have put diamonds on the floor."*

Amongst all the nonsense, I have mentioned a number of specific words to beware of; here I add one more. Another word to be wary of is "specialise". The Reed recruitment agency says it *"specialises in temporary, permanent and contract roles"*. Can you specialise in such a comprehensive range of employments? Specialise surely means to focus on specific things rather than do absolutely everything. A company can offer a wide range of services, but if it truly specialises then strictly it will focus on a limited range. Words such as this do tend to be thrown around just to impress.

If you keep chickens and buy any Poultry Shield to keep their little feathers free of nasty red mites then do be very careful how you use it, as it claims it *"Eliminates all organic matter"*. If your hen house is made of wood then that's that gone for ever, along with much of the surrounding environment. Mind you, the red mites should stand no chance. Anything poisonous always needs care. Most of us do not drink kitchen cleaning products or indeed anything of that sort; to be fair the warning notices on such containers are usually very clear. It is no surprise, therefore, to find Sainsbury's selling toilet cleaner that says *"If swallowed, rinse out mouth and seek medical attention"*. This is amongst a variety of other text making it very clear that this is not for consumption, so it is surprising that just below the warnings it also says: *"This product is suitable for use by vegetarians"*. Maybe that sort of diet gives you a cast iron constitution, or maybe a vegetarian diet leads to your needing a very special kind of cleaner to use after your ablutions – the mind boggles.

University exam paper:
No text is printed on this page.
This is surely a totally unnecessary waste of ink,
and anyway it's untrue.

Items inappropriately forbidden to children have already been mentioned, but this deserves to get in too: a simple anniversary card, surely a pretty hazardless object, carries the warning *"Not suitable for children under 3 years"*. In an ASDA supermarket, one counter displays a sign saying: *"If you would like a price for our turkeys, please see a frozen assistant for information"*. What would Health and Safety have to say about such terrible working conditions? Perhaps it's to get customers feeling sympathy for the poor souls and letting their guard down to greater persuasion.

Sitting at the computer getting these words down, I have paused on a regular basis and occasionally had a cup of tea and a snack. During one such break I discovered Walkers Sensations, a posh crisp which I find I love in the Southern Barbecue flavour and a bag of which was unaccountably hidden in the kitchen cupboard. They are very good; they are also, I see, among a number of products expecting us to be impressed by the fact that they use *"real ingredients"*. I know we live in a world of matrix-like simulated reality, but I don't think you can make crisps with anything *other* than real ingredients. There are not many imaginary potatoes and even if there were more, it would be a problem getting them onto the production line. This brand also says, rather confusingly, that it contains *"No artificial flavour enhancers"*, but then lists *"Flavourings"* and *"Smoke Flavouring"* along with a list of other things that must add to the taste.

Just for fun, I actually wrote to Walkers about this. First someone telephoned me and wanted to know why I wanted to know. On hearing that I was writing about them, they promised to reply in writing, which they duly did. Well, I say they did: they actually passed it to their Public Relations Consultants and paid them to write to me. What did they say? I quote:

> *In response to your query, we use the term 'made with real ingredients' to illustrate that Sensations do not include any artificial flavours, colours or additives in their ingredients. All the flavourings used in these crisps, including the smoke flavourings, are not artificial flavour enhancers, but are types of natural flavouring, made from natural sources – such as vanilla extract, lime oil or garlic powder.*
>
> *We trust this answers your query, and thank you for taking the time to contact us.*

So there you are. What does this make you think? Me, while I acknowledge that they can write what they like, it seems that having to explain that what appears on their packet should not be taken literally but needs some subtitles, as it were, is not really very good communication. From their point of view it is actually selling themselves short – I think many people may take "real" to mean, well, real, and then wonder just as I did. It's not so much that the statement is dishonest, indeed perish the thought: when I looked up the Public Relations Consultant's website, it said *"We believe that honesty earns trust"*. So the ingredients must be real. But we knew that; rather it's that the text is simply unclear. Nevertheless, I don't think I have eaten anything else with real smoke in it before; but maybe that's not what they meant.

Something to think about as you crunch; but it must be said that these crisps do go very well with a cold beer. Good heavens I hope my beer is brewed with something real, but if it isn't then maybe I will not be told by her indoors not to have another "because it will make you fat". I presume unreal ingredients would make for the ultimate diet. Maybe we should expect the imminent launch of a whole new range of non-fattening food products.

No access for vehicles over 7.5 tonnes except for access

says a road sign. This is so wrong it may actually *attract* large trucks; I see them now in convoy towards Cirencester where this notice is reported displayed.

When is a hazard not a hazard? Certainly in this case: "*Caution – this product moves during use*" says the label. Well, it would, the notice was on a child's scooter. In similar vein this warning "*Extremely flammable – do not use near fire or flame*" sounds like a sensible one, but it is on a cigarette lighter that is designed specifically to *produce* a flame. Better not carry two of them. Flames really can be dangerous, but what is one to make of this: *"Warning: potatoes – handle with care"*? There must be a mutant strain of carnivorous potatoes roaming the country, attacking those of us intent on turning them into chips. A garden centre grows its own blackberries and sells the plants. As these are described as *"non-thornless plants"* you can certainly expect a few pricks along the way. If some blackberries have thorns and other varieties do not, I wonder what exactly they meant. Also in the garden, Miracle-Gro Fruit & Vegetable Concentrated Plant Food is entirely open and comprehensive, I think, in describing its contents. These are listed as *"Nitrogen (N); phosphorus pentoxide (P2O2) and potassium oxide (K2O)"*. In much bolder type it says the product is *"100 per cent CHEMICAL FREE"*. Bad, bad, bad – what does it all consist of then and why put your spurious claim in capital letters? Another one for the naughty step.

Regarding ingredients in another product area, Newton Blueberry Balance tea has in it: *"Hibiscus, Rosehips, Apples, Echinacea Herb, Echinacia root, Flavourings, Orange Peel, Elderberries and Cinnamon"*. Again this seems like a comprehensive and openly displayed list, but the name clearly describes it as *"Blueberry"*... and yet it appears not to contain any! That's rather like selling a car with no wheels. Unless there is something here I do not understand, this is surely both odd and outrageous. Other products may be the same for all I know: orange juice with no oranges, spearmint toothpaste with no spearmint and leather shoes that have not been within a million miles of a cow. Makes you wonder.

This next one, too, could be described as a case of a missing ingredient. It's one that should apparently suit single ladies: an online advertisement pops up on screen saying *"The new way to shop for men... open 24/7, free shipping"*. So any time of the day or night availability and he comes to you, it would seem; rather disappointingly this turns out to be a site selling men's clothes.

A Puma shoe box is marked:
Average contents 2

Continuing the theme of ingredients, Co-operative stores sell smoked trout. On one 150 gram pack it lists the contents as *"Farmed trout (96 per cent) and Salt"*, with the salt explained as being *"1.3 grams per 100 grams"*. This sounds pure and good – but do the maths: what does the missing stuff in there consist of? Something seems not to be listed. Could be they have identified dark matter and are about to revolutionise physics.

Sometimes there are wording errors that annoy only the pedants. Top of the list are supermarkets that have checkouts labelled as for *"10 items or less"*, and round my way they compound the error by letting people with far more than 10 items check out there... just in front of me. It's *soooo* annoying. Stop it, and change those signs to "10 items or *fewer*" please. Significant numbers of kids already evidently leave school without appropriate reading and writing skills and this sort of thing does not help.

Other words and phrases sound good but may mean little. A phrase like *"hair care technology"* may sound good and be made to stand out in an advertisement too, but what does it mean? Such phrases are rarely explained. It's just not clear: maybe it describes something important and useful that makes a shampoo special and good. But maybe it just means they mix a few things in a bucket and stick it in a posh bottle.

A lack of precision is all around. Albeit these florescent light bulbs were bought from a market stall, but this does not really excuse their box saying *"Saves approx. 80 per cent more energy than a standard light bulb"*. Even in a bright light that is wholly unclear. On a UHT semi-skimmed milk bottle it says: *"Nothing added, nothing taken away"*; is it semi-skimmed or not, one wonders. And this changes the rules of physics: chamois leather cloths sold to clean your car are described thus: *"Soaks up water like a magnet"*. Presumably for cars sprinkled with iron filings. I guess we do know what this means, but it sounds funny and thus perhaps misses the mark.

If you want to add comments to the BBC News website, you need to register first. It says: *"We ask for date of birth to help improve the online safety of our young bbc.co.uk members. Once you have told us your date of birth, you will need to email us if you want to change it".* Presumably the people who do that are contacting the right site – it really would be news. *National Geographic* magazine offers those taking out a subscription various gifts. One such is a *"full size world map".* Great, but imagine the envelope needed to dispatch it. The description of the offer concludes, *"FREE when we receive your payment";* I suppose no one can blame them for not wanting to meet that dispatch cost until they have your money, but then it's not free!

Next, and this is impossible either way, there is *"slow setting, instant glue"* – one or the other seems more likely. But perhaps I may end this chapter with something of an introspective nature. It is also another clear example of description that seems to use the right words, but does so in a way that produces an odd result. When this book was published, I listed it with the Authors' Licensing and Collecting Society (ALCS). This body pays writers when their material is copied with permission (if you are reading this book in a library, for instance, a record is kept should you decide to copy a few pages and – eventually – it will add to the modest sum ALCS pay me each year. But I cannot resist adding that if you are reading this in a library – go out at once and buy a copy!). It is a worthy body, then, and one that has a website I must log onto occasionally. When I do so, I am asked to enter my *"memorable word"*. What's that? In my case it's FD68622B; and I always need to look it up.

Seriously... be warned

The incidences of the kind of errors that are quoted here seem almost endless; so too do the notes drawing attention to them. Going back to the vexed question of whether or not things that should not contain nuts do in fact contain nuts, I saw a letter to my local newspaper, *The Essex Chronicle,* only the other day, bizarrely reprimanding an item in last week's edition and saying that the recipe for squirrel stew should have included the warning *"may contain nuts"*.

We must be ever watchful and individually ever on our guard as we assess whether or not to buy a particular product or not. For example, do you want to buy invisible thread? Tesco apparently sells it, though when I noticed this the space behind the label was apparently empty; I was not sure whether they had it in stock or not.

This review has been, in part, a bit of fun. But there are lessons to be drawn and a few more pages, and examples, to go.

AFTERWORD

"One should not aim at being possible to understand,
but at being impossible to misunderstand."

Quintilian

THE QUOTATION ABOVE GOES BACK to Roman times and is my favourite comment on communications. Everyone concerned with telling the world about their organisation and their product should bear it in mind. It is often said that the customer is king. Yet all the examples in this book are evidence of the customer not being regarded in that way. It reminds me of the story of the marketer who changed career and became a policeman. Asked why, he replied that he liked it because "in this job the customer is always wrong". Only in one situation, perhaps, do we want as little done for us as possible – when we visit the dentist. From the customers' point of view we want to be respected, we want good service and we want clear communication; and finally a product that works – or in modern, ad-inspired language, "does what it says on the tin".

The market place used to be simple. When entrepreneurial Neanderthals were trading axe heads – *Three for the price of two and I'll throw in a spare handle –*

in exchange for, say, a week's supply of mammoth pie, there was little choice. Mammoth pie might not have been the gastronomic treat of the age, but waiting around for deep pan pizza to be invented was going to leave you very hungry. Much later on, when Henry Ford started selling his cars, it was said you could have one in any colour you wanted as long as it was black. He sold them in their thousands.

Now there is huge choice. Huge: I went onto the Amazon website as I wrote the word "huge" and just looked up a couple of products at random. They offer 15,109 different watches; and that's just for men. What about cameras? There is a choice of nearly four and a half thousand digital cameras. And all that is just from one supplier. I repeat: the choice available is huge. If we could measure it in elephants it would be a whole herd and a bit.

Label on Tesco's own brand organic milk:
Contains milk

This presents two problems. The first one is for those wanting us to buy things. They have to tell us about it and, given that everyone is exposed to hundreds of promotional messages every single day, they must tell us stridently to have any chance at all of being heard.

As an old (and as far as I know anonymous) poem puts it:

> *The codfish lays a thousand eggs*
> *The homely hen lays one.*
> *The codfish never cackles*
> *To tell you what she's done.*
> *And so we scorn the codfish*
> *While the humble hen we prize*
> *Which only goes to show you*
> *That it pays to advertise.*

Advertising is everywhere – you may have noticed – on television, in the press, on the internet... even on boxes of matches and the side of the space shuttle. It has been well described (by Stephen Leacock), who said: "*Advertising may be described as the science of arresting human intelligence long enough to get money from it.*" So do be warned, these messages are designed to stop *your* intelligence dead in its tracks and hook you, and they would not be doing their job if they were not replete with glowing terms and with words like new, improved, better, classic, guaranteed, special and many more. Incidentally, how can so many things be "new *and* improved"? And Tesco sell "*New, improved Swarfega Original*"? While on the subject of things being billed as new, another item worth a mention is Amcal Paracetamol painkillers: they come in a box that says "*New Formula*" on the front. But the ingredients are lists merely as *"Each tablet contains Paracetamol 500mg"* so what part of it in any way consists of a "new" formula? Again, this seems especially bad on a medical product, albeit just a simple headache pill. It is difficult to keep up with all this.

> The Bath Belle shower cap advises users to:
> **Place shower cap over head to prevent it from getting wet.**

But for the originators of such messages the danger is that perhaps if you call a spade a spade you won't last long in the world of advertising. You must embellish to survive and, as we have seen, doing so can create some odd messages, especially when – as often seems to be the case – it is done without thought, checking or a reasonable knowledge of the English language. This is no excuse. I should not have been able to write this book and I hope as a result of it standards may improve.

But there is a second problem. We, the customers, need advertising in all its forms. Without it we would not know what is available and if we did know of something we would know very little about it. Of course we say we don't like it and we record television programmes so that we can zap over the commercial breaks, but don't make the mistake of believing you are immune to advertising's wiles. An old story linked to one of the best known advertising slogans of all time makes the point. A researcher is asking people in pubs about their drinking habits. "Are you drinking Guinness because of their advertising?" they ask one customer. "Certainly not", replies the man "what do you take me for – that sort of thing doesn't fool me", adding "I drink Guinness because it's good for me". Unlikely perhaps, but it makes a good point – advertising is hard to ignore.

And, as I have said, we need it. Despite electric lawnmowers being sold with flex labelled *"for inside use only"*, despite being told nonsense measurements such as boxes made of *"at least 100 per cent recycled paper"* or a swimming pool thermometer boasting it goes down to minus 30C; despite being offered bottles of *"no-calorie water"* when no water contains any calories, and despite Wild Blueberry Yoghurt explaining that the blueberries it contains come from *"selected farms"* and are therefore not wild at all, we do need these messages. We may twitch at being told our life membership of something expires in six months, or that we should not switch on our carpet cleaner *"without any person nearby"* and we worry when we see a notice in a police car at London's Heathrow airport saying *"Explosive police dog"*. We need to see that last one if only to give it a wide berth.

Sign on gate:

Large savage dogs enter at your own risk

In the United Kingdom, that august body the Advertising Standards Authority pledges to keep all advertising legal, decent and honest. Those who really transgress, advertising two-penny tablets to drop into a can of water to make cheap petrol or promising that men using their deodorant will be in bed with a nubile young lady within the hour, will be severely reprimanded. Sorry, only the first one of those is true, there are evidently a number of toiletry products that promise instant nymphomaniac and do so unchallenged. So it must be true. One must presume that the said Authority ignores nonsensical claims such as the Philips hair dryer which promises, oddly for a hair dryer, to leave your hair *"moisture rich"*. Anyway, some protection from major transgressions does exist and similar bodies operate in other countries.

But no one seems to take sanctions against the myriad of small inaccuracies, the plethora of miswritten descriptions, the many nonsensical numbers or, amongst them all, the small sneaky deceptions that are slipped in and aimed at increasing the volume of ill-considered purchases made. Hence this book: it aims to show such things up, it pokes well deserved fun at them and at their authors, some of whom would remain rich if brains were taxed. It also acts as a warning to read carefully and act accordingly.

Be warned

So watch out for those who cannot even describe their product in plain English, who are terminally number blind, who don't check what they have written or who think so little of you that they believe that you will immediately purchase anything described as new, improved and exceptional, especially if it is unique to you or, better still *very* unique to you (the latter phrase being especially favoured though, for the record, nothing can be very unique).

Read carefully, especially the small print and between the lines; check, ask questions, phone a friend – whatever it takes to be clear what something really means. Be especially careful when figures are involved and even more so if they involve decimals, percentages and, above all, money. It's your money they are after.

I'll address the last word to those writing the sort of nonsense featured here, and do so in the form of a sign seen in one customer-orientated store some years back:

WARNING: CUSTOMERS ARE PERISHABLE

So they are. We rarely *have* to buy from someone; there are nearly always alternatives. Be warned out there, if we do not like the way you address us we can and will vote with our feet and walk away. The ultimate penalty for wielding weapons of mass disinformation is that we ignore you.

Seriously – be warned:

Everyone wanting to sell to you wants to make what they say about their product as beguiling as possible. They love certain words that are believed to create a good "purchase-friendly" feeling, however inappropriately they may be used. Such so-called "magic words" include: free, guaranteed, new, announcing, you, now, today, win, easy, save, at once, unique, timely, respected, reliable, genuine, opportunity, low-cost, save, upgrade, enhance, and fresh.

The list could go on, but you get the idea. Any one of these, and particularly combinations of them, may herald a good deal or provide useful early warning of a trap to get you to spend as much as possible while applying the minimum of thought to the transaction. Take care.

POSTSCRIPT

"Someone else's ignorance is bliss."

Jack Vance

I HAVE BEEN PRETTY SCATHING about many of the errors recorded here, though rightly so, perhaps especially regarding those that may engender real confusion, inconvenience or even danger. If you take it literally that Growing Success mouse killer is *"For use only as an amateur mouse killer"* you will leave all those pesky professional mice to run riot and eat you out of house and home.

That said, let me admit that realistically some errors are perhaps inevitable. Some have no mischievous intent and have simply slipped through. The authors of such are no doubt contrite if their errors are pointed out to them and, as was said at the start, many of the words quoted here have no doubt now been corrected or dropped.

I am sure I am not immune to all this. I wrote this carefully. I checked it carefully, as did my editor; the proofs were read (again carefully) by at least three people and for all I know the publisher may have shown it to many more; if you find paw marks on the pages then it is likely because the office cat had a look too.

165

Incidentally, considering the process of checking (or rather not checking) reminds me of something mentioned in the Introduction: the computer manual I have by my desk with the following boxed paragraph on its title page:

This manual has been carefully to remove any errors.

One feels for whomever proof read this, they could not have missed out a worse word, but I digress.

Despite all this checking, I would not be surprised if you find an error, or tow (sic) here. So I'll end with an apology and a request. If you find an error, even if it is a simply slip of the typing finger, then I apologise – everyone involved was very careful as I say. Finally if you feel the need to write to us and point a typo out, please don't be too harsh – and certainly do not let it stop you from buying more copies of the book to give to all your friends.

Website: "**Proof-Reading-Service.net provides professional proofreading services exclusively for professors, lecturers, post-doc's and research students and businesses**". *No one is immune – and here it's those tricky apostrophes again.*

Note: in many books featuring collected information like this, there is a traditional request to let the author know if you discover more. This is not always well expressed: way back, the magazine *Macworld* classically asked for tips to be sent to Apple saying "*Send your tips to quanda@macworld.co.uk We cannot make personal replies, so please do not include a stamped addressed envelope*". Evidently, at that time, even the mighty Apple did not quite get the internet. In this case there are just so many examples of this kind of stuff that I won't do that – so thank you but just keep any further examples to yourself or write to the originator; they deserve to be annoyed.

THE AUTHOR

 PATRICK FORSYTH has a background in marketing and worked initially in publishing before moving into management consultancy and training. Alongside that he has written a host of how-to books on business, management, careers and self-help and had his books translated into 24 languages. He has done all sorts of things in the business world from speaking at conferences to acting as advisor on the production of training films; none of which things are of any great import here.

More importantly he loves writing and is extending his subject matter beyond business topics. He loves to travel and has recently written two travel books, one of which, *A land like none you know*, is a light hearted account of a journey through Burma and available from the author. For more information email *patrick@touchstonetc.freeserve.co.uk* or check out *www.patrickforsyth.com*

He also writes about writing in *Writing Magazine*, gives talks about non-fiction writing and travel writing. Patrick lives overlooking the River Blackwater in Maldon and his writing is interrupted on a regular basis by Sue saying "Are you at that computer again?"

Lightning Source UK Ltd.
Milton Keynes UK
UKOW020615131011

180185UK00004B/3/P